Financial Literacy Basics:

Calculating the Cost of College & Understanding Student Loans

Financial Literacy Basics:

Calculating the Cost of College & Understanding Student Loans

2022 Edition

GREY HOUSE PUBLISHING

FINANCIAL RATINGS SERIES

WeissRatings
& Grey House Publishing

https://greyhouse.weissratings.com

Grey House Publishing
4919 Route 22, PO Box 56
Amenia, NY 12501-0056
(800) 562-2139

Weiss Ratings
4400 Northcorp Parkway
Palm Beach Gardens, FL 33410
(561) 627-3300

Published by Grey House Publishing, Inc., located at 4919 Route 22, Amenia, NY 12501; telephone 518-789-8700. Grey House Publishing neither guarantees the accuracy of the data contained herein nor assumes any responsibility for errors, omissions or discrepancies. Grey House Publishing accepts no payment for listing; inclusion in the publication of any organization, agency, institution, publication, service or individual does not imply endorsement of the publisher.

Grey House Publishing

2022 Edition
ISBN: 978-1-64265-890-3

Table of Contents

Welcome!

Grey House Publishing and Weiss Ratings are proud to announce the fifth edition of *Financial Literacy Basics*. Each volume in this series provides readers with easy-to-understand guidance on how to manage their finances. Designed for those who are just starting out, as well as those who may need help handling their finances, the volumes in this series outline, step-by-step, how to make the most of your money, which pitfalls to avoid, what to watch out for, and the necessary tools to make sure you are fully equipped to manage your finances.

Each of these eight volumes focus on specific ways to take the guesswork out of financial planning—how to stick to a budget, how to manage debt, how to buy a car or rent an apartment, how to calculate the cost of college, and how to start saving for retirement—all information necessary to get started on your financial future. Each volume is devoted to a specific topic. Combined, they provide you with a full range of helpful information on how to best manage your money. Individual volumes are:

- How to **Make and Stick to a Budget**
- How to **Manage Debt**
- Starting a **401(k)**
- Understanding **Health Insurance** Plans
- **Renting an Apartment** & Understanding **Renters Insurance**
- Understanding the **Cost of College**, **Student Loans**& How to Pay Them Back
- **Buying a Car** & Understanding **Auto Insurance**
- What to Know About **Checking Accounts**

Filled with valuable information that includes helpful, hands-on worksheets and planners, these volumes are designed to point you toward a solid financial future with clear suggestions, supportive guidance and easy-to-follow dos and don'ts.

Financial Literacy Basics: Calculating the Cost of College & Understanding Student Loans

Part 1: Calculating the Cost of a College Education

Investing in Your Future

Student loans can be important to your future. They help you get an education, which can help you start a career and earn more money. Young adults with a bachelor's degree are more likely to find full-time work and generally earn more than those without a bachelor's degree, according to the U.S. Department of Education.

But taking on education debt means you are committed to repaying the loans. Various student loans may have very different terms. Before you sign for a loan, be sure you understand what kind of loan you are getting and when and how you must repay it.

Also be sure you are borrowing only what you need, because you will have to pay interest on the loan.

Explore Your Career Options

Keep in mind that students who want to further their education have many more options than a traditional four-year degree. For some, a two-year Associate's degree is the right way to go, or maybe a trade or vocational school will be the right path to a rewarding and well-paying career.

To get an idea of what you might earn in various occupations, look at employment prospects at the U.S. Department of Labor's *Occupation Outlook Handbook* (https://www.bls.gov/ooh),and talk to your school counselors to find out what recent graduates from your program of study are earning.

You can also use the *Occupational Outlook Handbook* to find jobs based on entry-level education, or jobs that have a high number of projected openings.

You can search for jobs that offer apprenticeships, on-the-job training, or non-degree certificate programs like trade schools and vocational schools. For those who want to minimize student debt, or want to start working right out of high school, there are several options to choose from.

Below are examples of career options and the 2020 median annual salary, based on the entry-level education required.

High School Diploma & On-the-Job Apprenticeship*

- Elevator Installers & Repairers: $88,540

- Electricians: $56,900

- Plumbers, Pipefitters & Steamfitters: $56,330

If an apprenticeship is not available in your area, these careers can also be pursued through a vocational or trade school program.

Vocational School & Trade School Programs

- Aircraft Mechanics: $66,680

- HVAC Technicians: $50,590

- Firefighters: $52,500

- License Practical Nurse (LPN): $48,820

- Automotive Mechanics: $44,050

- Emergency Medical Technicians: $36,650

Two-Year Associate's Degree

- Air Traffic Controllers: $130,420

- Dental Hygienists: $77,090

- Physical Therapy Assistants: $49,970

- Architectural & Civil Drafters: $57,960

Four-Year Bachelor's Degree

- Financial Manager: $134,180

- Registered Nurse (RN): $75,330

- Web Designer: $77,200

- Social Workers: $51,760

Use the Occupational Statistics table in the Appendix to view data on more potential career paths. Knowing what you will be earning when you graduate, and how many years it will take you to graduate, will help you budget for potential student loans and make sure you still have enough to live on.

How Much Does a College Education Cost?

The cost of a college education can vary greatly depending on the institution you attend, how much financial aid you receive and how many years you attend college.

Here are the average annual costs for tuition and fees for the 2021/2022 school year[1]:

- Private 4-Year Not-for-Profit Colleges & Universities: **$38,070**

- Public 4-Year Colleges & Universities (Out-of-State): **$27,560**

- Public 4-Year Colleges & Universities (In-State): **$10,740**

- Public 2-Year Colleges & Universities (In-District): **$3,800**

- Private For-Profit Colleges & Universities: **$15,780**

There are many other expenses that college students should plan for, on top of tuition and fees.

- **Room & Board** ranges from $9,330 to $13,620 per year

Once you add up the tuition, fees, and room & board, the breakdown of total yearly costs by type of institution is:

- Private 4-Year Not-for-Profit Colleges & Universities: **$50,580**

- Public 4-Year Colleges & Universities (Out-of-State): **$39,510**

- Public 4-Year Colleges & Universities (In-State): **$22,690**

- Public 2-Year Colleges & Universities (In-District):**$13,130**

- Private For-Profit: **$15,780** (includes cost of tuition only)

But, that's not all. You'll have to budget for additional costs:

- **Books & Supplies** range from $1,240 to $1,460 per year

- **Transportation** ranges from $1,060 to $1,840 per year

- **Other Expenses** range from $1,810 to $2,400 per year

Since the costs can vary so greatly, you'll want to weigh your options carefully when choosing your career path and your school.

[1]Source: Trends in College Pricing, https://trends.collegeboard.org/college-pricing

More Education Usually Means Higher Earnings

On average, higher degrees of education result in higher earnings. Considering a 40-year career, these are the lifetime earnings by level of education:

- Doctoral Degree: **$3,920,800**

- Professional Degree: **$3,937,440**

- Master's Degree: **$3,213,600**

- Bachelor's Degree: **$2,714,400**

- Associate's Degree: **$1,951,040**

- Some College, No Degree: **$1,824,160**

- High School Diploma: **$1,624,480**

- Less than a High School Diploma: **$1,287,520**

That means that someone with a Bachelor's degree will earn more than $1,000,000 more in their lifetime than someone with a high school diploma.

Your lifetime earning potential should be factored in when considering whether or not to go on to higher education after high school.

Earnings and unemployment rates by educational attainment, 2020

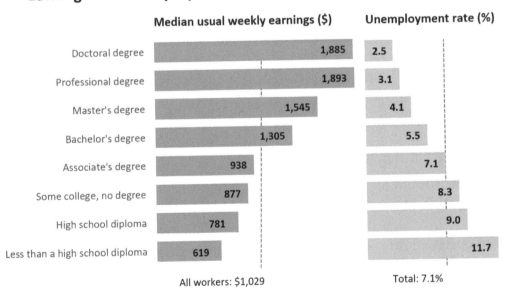

	Median usual weekly earnings ($)	Unemployment rate (%)
Doctoral degree	1,885	2.5
Professional degree	1,893	3.1
Master's degree	1,545	4.1
Bachelor's degree	1,305	5.5
Associate's degree	938	7.1
Some college, no degree	877	8.3
High school diploma	781	9.0
Less than a high school diploma	619	11.7
	All workers: $1,029	Total: 7.1%

Note: Data are for persons age 25 and over. Earnings are for full-time wage and salary workers.
Source: U.S. Bureau of Labor Statistics, Current Population Survey.

Choosing a School

There is a wide variety of schools available for higher education.

Options include:

- **Four-Year Colleges & Universities**

- **Two-Year Colleges & Universities**

- **Vocational Schools**

- **Trade Schools**

- **Career Schools**

- **Online Schools**

- **Graduate Schools**

Financial assistance programs and requirements can vary from school to school. Plus, not all colleges and career schools participate in federal student aid programs. Always check with your school to find out which financial aid programs will be available to you there.

Understanding your career goals and options (and their earning potential) will help you find a college or career school that meets your needs.

The U.S. Department of Education's college search tool, **College Navigator** can be found here: https://nces.ed.gov/collegenavigator. This site helps you find colleges and career schools that fit your needs. You can search for schools by location, degrees offered, programs/majors, tuition and fees, setting, size, and much more.

The U.S. Department of Education also provides a **Net Price Calculator**. The net price is the amount that a student pays to attend an institution in a single academic year after subtracting scholarships and grants the student receives. Scholarships and grants are forms of financial aid that a student does not have to pay back. Visit https://collegecost.ed.gov/net-price to get started. You can enter in the schools that you are interested in and get a real sense of what the cost will be for each school.

Choosing the right school involves a variety of factors including your interests, career goals, and financial situation, as well as the school's cost, size and location, and admissions requirements.

Your education is a major investment, so find out as much information as you can—before you enroll. And because each school will most likely offer different financial aid packages, you should consider applying to more than one school in order to compare costs.

Estimate Your Financial Aid Availability and the Cost of Attending Your School

The U.S. Department of Education's Office of Federal Student Aid makes a free tool available so you can estimate your eligibility for federal financial aid.

Visit https://studentaid.gov/aid-estimator/ to start your federal student aid estimate.

This estimator is recommended for high school juniors, but even parents of younger students can use the estimator to receive early estimates, create scenarios based on future earnings, and then establish college funding strategies.

Adult students also can use the student aid estimator to get an idea of what aid they might receive.

The estimator asks financial and other questions that are used to estimate your federal student aid eligibility. You may be able to answer most of the questions easily, but some of the questions will ask you to reference your personal records (for instance,

your federal tax information or your bank statements).

Be sure to answer all the questions on the federal student aid estimator, even if you have to estimate or guess.

When you complete the federal student aid estimator, the screen displays a worksheet to help you determine the net cost of attending your chosen school.

Here's what to expect on the worksheet:

- At the top of the page, enter the school's cost of attendance.

- Next, sources of college funding are listed, including your estimated Federal Pell Grant amount (if any), Federal Work-Study amount (based on the average nationally), and maximum Direct Subsidized Loan and Direct Unsubsidized Loan eligibility.

- You will be asked to fill in the amounts of state and college aid and private scholarships you expect (or hope) to get.

- Once you select "Calculate," the federal student aid estimator summarizes the cost, the total aid entered, and the difference (the net cost of attending college). Your estimated Expected Family

Contribution (EFC) also appears. You can compare schools by changing the variables: the cost of attendance; state aid options; the amount of aid available from the school, etc.

- The School Costs Comparison Worksheet on the next page is another way to estimate the cost of attending your school.

SCHOOL COSTS COMPARISON WORKSHEET

	School #1	School #2	School #3
School name			
Federal school code			
FAFSA deadline			

A. COSTS

	School #1	School #2	School #3
Tuition and fees			
Room and board			
Books and supplies			
Transportation			
Miscellaneous/personal			
Additional costs			
Total cost of attendance (add up this section, write in total)			

B. NEED

	School #1	School #2	School #3
Total cost of attendance (write in total from section A)			
Expected family contribution (EFC)			
Total financial need (subtract family contribution from total cost of attendance)			

C. LOANS & GRANTS

	School #1	School #2	School #3
Federal Pell Grant			
Federal SEOG Grant			
Federal TEACH Grant			
Institutional aid			
State aid			
Private scholarships			
Veterans educational benefits			
Employment			
Federal Work Study			
Loans			
Federal Perkins Loan			
Federal Direct Subsidized Loan			
Federal Direct Unsubsidized Loan			
Federal Direct PLUS Loan			
Institutional Loan			
Private Loan			
Other			
Total financial aid (add up this section, write in total)			

D. SUMMARY

	School #1	School #2	School #3
Total financial need (write in total from section B)			
Total financial aid (write in total from Section C)			
Additional Out-of-Pocket Costs (subtract total financial aid from total financial need)			

Part 2: Applying for Student Loans, Grants & Scholarships

Applying for Student Loans

Once you have compared the costs and made your decision on which school to attend, first and foremost, visit your school's financial aid office. The staff at the financial aid office will help you apply for and receive student loans, grants, scholarships and other types of financial aid.

If you decide to take out a loan, make sure you understand who is making the loan and the terms and conditions of the loan. Student loans can come from the federal government or from private sources such as a bank or financial institution.

Before you take out a loan, it's important to understand that a loan is a legal obligation that you will be responsible for repaying with interest. You may not have to begin repaying your student loans right away, but you shouldn't wait to understand your responsibilities as a borrower.

Types of Student Loans

Student loans may be federal or private.

Federal Student Loans

Federal student loans come from the federal government and have many advantages. Repayment terms are often more flexible, and interest rates are usually lower than loans from private sources (financial institutions such as banks). As long as you remain a full-time student, you will not have to begin repaying federal student loans while still attending college, but in some cases you may have to make payments on private loans before you graduate.

Federal student loans have fixed interest rates and are usually subsidized, which means the government pays the interest while you are a student. You usually do not need a cosigner, and in most cases will not need a credit check. Your interest may be tax deductible, and you may be able to consolidate federal loans or choose from several repayment plans. You may also be able to temporarily postpone payment if you are having financial difficulties, and in certain professions some of your federal student loans may be forgiven.

There are four kinds of **Direct Federal Loans:**

- **Direct subsidized loans**, which are for students with financial need enrolled in undergraduate or career school programs;

- **Direct unsubsidized loans**, which are for students in undergraduate, graduate, and professional programs who do not demonstrate financial need;

- **Direct PLUS Loans**, which may cover educational expenses that other loans do not. These loans are made to the student and parents and require a credit check for parents; and

- **Direct Consolidation Loans**, which may enable students to combine federal student loans into one loan, eliminating the need to make multiple payments.

You may also qualify for **State Loans**, either in the state where you live or in the state where you go to school. Contact your school's financial aid office or visit your state's Department of Education website for more information.

Private Student Loans

Private loans are similar to personal loans. The financial institution to which you apply will look at your credit history to decide if you are eligible for an education loan and to set the interest rate. The terms of federal student loans—including interest rates—are generally better than private education loans. You will probably benefit most if you turn to private sources only if federal loans will not cover your education costs. Some lenders may charge fees, which could offset low interest rates and actually cost you more.

Apply for Federal Student Loans First

Loans made by the federal government, called federal student loans, usually offer borrowers lower interest rates and have more flexible repayment options than loans from banks or other private sources.

Federal student loans offer many benefits compared to other options you may consider when paying for college:

- The interest rate on federal student loans is almost always lower than that on private loans—and much, much lower than that on a credit card!

- You don't need a credit check or a cosigner to get most federal student loans.

- You don't have to begin repaying your federal student loans until after you leave college or drop below half-time.

- If you demonstrate financial need, you can qualify to have the government pay your interest while you are in school.

- Federal student loans offer flexible repayment plans and options to postpone your loan payments if you're having trouble making payments.

- If you work in certain jobs, you may be eligible to have a portion of your federal student loans forgiven if you meet certain conditions.

How Much Money Can I Borrow in Federal Student Loans?

If you are an undergraduate student:

- $5,500 to $12,500 per year in Direct Subsidized Loans and Direct Unsubsidized Loans depending on certain factors, including your year in college.

If you are a graduate student:

- Up to $20,500 each year in Direct Unsubsidized Loans.

- The remainder of your college costs not covered by other financial aid in Direct PLUS Loans. Note: A credit check is required for a PLUS loan.

If you are a parent of a dependent undergraduate student:

- You can borrow the remainder of your child's college costs that are not covered by other financial aid with a Direct PLUS Loan.

The Application for Federal Student Aid: FAFSA

To apply for a federal student loan, you must complete and submit a Free Application for Federal Student Aid (FAFSA). The FAFSA application can be found here: https://studentaid.gov/h/apply-for-aid/fafsa

Based on the results of your FAFSA, your college or career school will send you a financial aid offer, which may include federal student loans. The financial aid office at your school will tell you how to accept all or a part of the loan.

Before you receive your loan funds, you will be required to:

- complete entrance counseling, to ensure you understand your obligation to repay the loan; and

- sign a Master Promissory Note (MPN), agreeing to the terms of the loan.

Contact the financial aid office at the school you are planning to attend for details regarding the process at your school.

In addition, many states and colleges use your FAFSA information to determine your eligibility for state and school aid, and some private financial aid providers may use your FAFSA information to determine whether you qualify for their aid.

If you don't fill out the FAFSA form, you could be missing out on a lot of financial aid. Even if you think your parents make too much money to qualify for financial aid, or that you are too old for financial aid, it is a good idea to apply anyway.

EVERYONE who's getting ready to go to college or career school should fill out the FAFSA form.

You can estimate what you will receive in federal student aid on the Federal Office of Student Aid's website using the following link: https://studentaid.gov/aid-estimator/

You have to fill out the FAFSA form every year you're in school in order to stay eligible for federal student aid.

Independent Students

A student's dependency status determines whose information they must report on the FAFSA form.

You are an independent student if you are: at least 24 years old; married;

a graduate or professional student; a veteran; a member of the armed forces; an orphan; a ward of the court; someone with legal dependents other than a spouse; an emancipated minor or someone who is homeless or at risk of becoming homeless.

If any of the above is true, then for federal student aid purposes, you will not provide information about your parents on the FAFSA form. If none of the above is true, you are considered dependent and must report your parents' information on the FAFSA form.

If a parent does not contribute to a student's education, refuses to file the FAFSA form, or does not claim the student as a dependent on their federal income tax returns, the student is still considered dependent, even if the student is totally self-sufficient.

Processing Your FAFSA Application

Your FAFSA information is shared with the colleges and/or career schools that you list on your application. The financial aid office at your school uses your information to figure out how much federal student aid you may receive at that school.

If the school has its own funds to use for financial aid, it might use your FAFSA information to determine your eligibility for that aid as well. Your school might also have other forms for you to fill out to get school aid, so check with the financial aid office to be sure.

Your information also goes to your state's higher education agency, as well as to agencies of the states where your chosen schools are located. Many states have financial aid funds that they give out based on FAFSA information.

That means that completing your FAFSA form helps you apply for federal, state, and school financial aid, all in one.

When your application is processed you will receive a Student Aid Report from the office of Federal Student Aid at the U.S. Department of Education, which is a summary of the FAFSA data you submitted.

If you applied for admission to a college or career school and have been accepted, and you listed that school on your FAFSA form, the school will calculate your aid and will send you an electronic or paper aid offer, sometimes called an award letter, telling you how much aid you're eligible for at the school. The timing of the aid offer varies from school to school and could be as early as winter (awarding for the following fall) or as late as immediately before you start school. It depends on when you apply and how the school prefers to schedule awarding of aid.

FAFSA Deadlines

In order to be considered for federal financial aid, you have to apply by the appropriate deadline.

Federal Student Aid

- For the 2022-2023 year, you must submit your FAFSA form by June 30, 2022.

- The FAFSA form is available each year on October 1 for the next school year. Some federal student aid programs have limited funds, however, that are awarded on a first-come first-serve basis, so be sure to apply as soon as you can once the FAFSA form is available for the year you'll be attending school.

State Student Aid

- You can find state deadlines at fafsa.gov. Note that several states have financial aid programs with limited funds and therefore have a deadline of "as soon as possible [after

the FAFSA form becomes available]."

College or Career School Aid

- Check the school's website or contact its financial aid office. School deadlines are usually early in the year (often in February or March, although some are even earlier now that the FAFSA form is available in October).

Other Financial Aid

- Some programs other than government or school aid also require that you fill out and submit the FAFSA form. For instance, you can't get certain private scholarships unless you're eligible for a Federal Pell Grant—and you can't find out whether you're eligible for a Pell Grant unless you fill out and submit the FAFSA form. If the private scholarship's application deadline is in early to mid-January, you'll need to submit your FAFSA form before that deadline.

Borrow Only What You Need

You should borrow only what you need. If your living expenses are not going to be as high as the amount estimated by your school, you have the right to turn down the loan or to request a lower loan amount. In their aid offer, the school will tell you how to do this.

Your Financial Aid Offer

When your school financial aid office sends you a financial aid offer, or an award letter, they will ask you to indicate which financial aid you want. Look carefully at your options and make an informed decision.

The rule is: accept free money first (scholarships and grants), then earned money (work-study), and then borrowed money (federal student loans). See below:

Order in Which to Accept Aid

1. Scholarships and grants

Make sure you understand the conditions you must meet. For instance, you might have to maintain a certain grade-point average in order to continue receiving a scholarship, or your TEACH Grant might turn into a loan if you don't teach for a certain number of years under specific circumstances.

2. Work-study

You don't have to pay the money back, but you do have to work for it, which means less time for studying. However, research has shown that students who work part-time jobs manage their time better than those who don't.

3. Federal student loans

You'll have to repay the money with interest. Subsidized loans don't start accruing (accumulating) interest until you leave school, so accept a subsidized loan before an unsubsidized loan.

4. Loans from your state government or your college

You'll have to repay the money with interest, and the terms of the loan might not be as good as those of a federal student loan. Be sure to read all the fine print before you borrow.

5. Private loans

You'll have to repay the money with interest, and the terms and conditions of the loan almost certainly will not be as good as those of a federal student loan.

How to Apply for Grants & Scholarships

Grants and scholarships are often called "gift aid" because they are free money—financial aid that doesn't have to be repaid. Grants are often need-based, which is based on a student's financial need, while scholarships are usually merit-based, which is based on a student's skill or ability.

Grants and scholarships can come from the federal government, your state government, your college or career school, or a private or nonprofit organization.

Do your research! Apply for ALL grants or scholarships that you might be eligible for, and be sure to meet application deadlines.

The U.S. Department of Education offers a variety of federal grants to students attending four-year colleges or universities, community colleges, and career schools.

Visit these websites for more information about these grants and scholarships.

- **Federal Pell Grants:**
  https://studentaid.gov/understand-aid/types/grants/pell

- **Federal Supplemental Educational Opportunity Grants (FSEOG):**
  https://studentaid.gov/understand-aid/types/grants/fseog

- **Teacher Education Assistance for College and Higher Education (TEACH) Grants:**
  https://studentaid.gov/understand-aid/types/grants/teach

- **Iraq and Afghanistan Service Grants:**
  https://studentaid.gov/understand-aid/types/grants/iraq-afghanistan-service

Program details and annual award figures for the grants listed above can be found here:
https://studentaid.gov/sites/default/files/federal-grant-programs.pdf

To apply for federal grants, you'll need to fill out the FAFSA form to get started.

A helpful list of Where to Find Financial Aid, Grants & Scholarships State by State is included in the appendix of this volume.

More Information About Scholarships

Scholarships are gifts. They don't need to be repaid. There are thousands of them, offered by schools, employers, individuals, private companies, nonprofits, communities, religious groups, and professional and social organizations.

Some scholarships for college are merit-based. You earn them by meeting or exceeding certain standards set by the scholarship-giver. Merit scholarships might be awarded based on academic achievement or on a combination of academics and a special talent, trait, or interest. Other scholarships are based on financial need.

You can learn about scholarships in several ways, including contacting the financial aid office at the school you plan to attend.

In addition, these free sources offer information about scholarships:

- A high school or TRIO (Upward Bound, Talent Search, or Student Support Service) counselor

- U.S. Department of Labor's FREE scholarship search tool available at https://www.careeronestop.org/toolkit/training/find-scholarships.aspx

- State grant agency website at https://www2.ed.gov/about/contacts/state/index.html

- Your library's reference section

- Foundations, religious or community organizations, local businesses, or civic groups

- Organizations (including professional associations) related to your field of interest

- Ethnicity-based organizations

- Your employer or your parents' employers

Each scholarship has its own requirements. The scholarship's website will indicate qualifications and how to apply. Make sure you read the application carefully, fill it out completely, and meet the application deadline.

A scholarship will affect your other student aid because all your student aid together can't be more than your cost of attendance at your college or career school. Let your school know if you've been awarded a scholarship so that the financial aid office can subtract that amount from your cost of attendance (and from certain other aid, such as loans, that you might have been offered). Then, any amount left can be covered by other financial aid for which you're eligible.

Work-Study Programs

Federal Work-Study programs provide part-time jobs for undergraduate and graduate students with financial need, allowing them to earn money to help pay education expenses. The program encourages community service work and work related to the student's course of study. These work-study programs:

- Provide part-time employment while you are enrolled in school;

- Are available to undergraduate, graduate, and professional students with financial need;

- Are available to full-time or part-time students; and

- Are administered by schools participating in the Federal Work-Study Program. Check with your school's financial aid office to find out if your school participates.

Jobs are available on campus and off campus. If you work on campus, you'll usually work for your school. If you work off campus, your employer will most likely be a private nonprofit organization or a public agency, and the work performed must be in the public interest, like city government, public schools, community hospitals, public libraries, community centers, day care centers, halfway houses, crisis centers, and summer camps.

Some schools have agreements with private for-profit employers for work-study jobs. These jobs usually must be relevant to your course of study. If you attend a proprietary school (i.e., a for-profit institution), there may be further restrictions on the types of jobs you can be assigned.

If you're interested in getting a Federal Work-Study job while you're enrolled in college or career school, make sure you apply for aid early. Funds are limited.

Your total work-study award depends on:

- when you apply;

- your level of financial need; and

- your school's funding level.

A Federal Work-Study job will earn you at least the current federal minimum wage. However, you may earn more depending on the type of work you do and the skills required for the position.

How you're paid depends partly on whether you're an undergraduate or graduate student. If you are an undergraduate student, you're paid by the hour. If you are a graduate or professional student, you may be paid by salary, which is a fixed amount based on the length of your employment.

Your school must pay you at least once a month. Your school must pay you directly unless you request that it deposit your pay directly to your bank account, or that it use the money to pay for your education-related costs.

The amount you earn can't exceed your total Federal Work-Study award. When assigning work hours, your employer or your school's financial aid office will consider your class schedule and your academic progress.

Accepting Your Aid Offer

Read and follow the directions in the aid offer or award letter. You might have to enter the amounts you're accepting in an online form and then submit the form. If you receive a paper aid offer, you might have to sign it and mail it back to the school.

Accepting a loan listed in the aid offer involves some additional steps, which vary depending on the type of loan you're receiving. Saying yes may be as simple as signing a promissory note— a contract between you and the lender that specifies terms and conditions of the loan.

If you take out a loan from the Direct Loan Program, the U.S. Department of Education will be your lender. By signing the promissory note, you are promising to repay your student loan. The financial aid office will guide you through the paperwork or direct you to StudentLoans.gov to sign the online Master Promissory Note.

When Will I Receive my Financial Aid?

Generally, your grant or loan will cover a full academic year and your school will pay out your money in at least two payments called disbursements.

For most grants and student loans, your school will receive your money and apply it to your tuition, fees, and room & board.   If there is money left over, they will give it to you to pay for additional educational expenses.

In most cases, your school must disperse your money at least once per term (semester, trimester, or quarter). Schools that don't use traditional terms such as semesters or quarters usually must disperse your money at least twice per academic year—for instance, at the beginning and midpoint of your academic year.

- If you're a parent taking out a Direct PLUS Loan to help pay for your child's education expenses, your loan funds will be disbursed according to the same type of schedule (usually, at least twice per academic year).

- If you're a first-year undergraduate student and a first-time borrower, you may have to wait 30 days after the first day of your enrollment period (semester, trimester, etc.) for your first disbursement. Check with your school to see whether this rule applies there.

- If you're a first-time borrower of a Direct Subsidized Loan or a Direct Unsubsidized Loan, you must complete entrance counseling before you receive your first loan disbursement. Similarly, if you are a graduate or professional student taking out a Direct PLUS Loan for the first time, you must complete entrance counseling before receiving your first disbursement. If you are a parent taking out a Direct PLUS Loan to help pay for your child's education, you will not be required to participate in entrance counseling.

How Will I Receive my Financial Aid?

Grants and Student Loans

Typically, the college first applies your grant or loan money toward your tuition, fees, and (if you live on campus) room and board. Any money left over is paid to you for other expenses. You might be able to choose whether the leftover money comes to you by check, cash, a credit to your bank account, or another method.

If your loan is disbursed but then you realize that you don't need the money after all, you may cancel your loan within 120 days of the disbursement, and no interest or fees will be charged.

Work-Study

Your school must pay you directly (for instance, by cash or check) unless you request that the school:

- send your payments directly to your bank account; or

- use the money to pay for education-related charges (such as tuition, fees, and room and board) on your student account.

Direct PLUS Loan/Parent (PLUS) Loans

In most cases, a child's school will disburse a parent's loan money by crediting it to the school to pay tuition, fees, room, board, and other authorized charges. If there is money left over, the school will return it to the parent or disburse the leftover money to the child.

If you take out a (student or parent) loan, the school will notify you in writing each time they disburse part of your loan money. At the same time,

they will provide information about how to cancel all or part of your disbursement if you find you no longer need the full amount. You also will receive a notice from your loan servicer confirming the disbursement.

Entrance Counseling

An entrance counseling session is designed to help you understand what it means to take out a federal student loan.

During entrance counseling, you will learn about the following:

- What a Direct Loan is and how the loan process works;

- Managing your education expenses;

- Other financial resources to consider to help pay for your education; and

- Your rights and responsibilities as a borrower.

How to Avoid Scholarship and Other Financial Aid Scams

Be careful. Make sure scholarship information and offers you receive are legitimate.

Remember that you don't have to pay to find scholarships or other financial aid.

The U.S. Department of Education[2] recommends these steps to help steer clear of financial aid and scholarship scams.

 Commercial financial aid advice services can cost well over $1,000. Charging for help or information that's available for free elsewhere is not fraudulent. However, if a company doesn't deliver what it promises, it's scamming you.

 If you're unsure whether to pay a company for help finding financial aid, stop and think for a minute: What's being offered? Is the service going to be worth your money? Do the claims seem too good to be true?

You might have heard or seen these claims at seminars, over the phone from telemarketers, or online:

 Buy now or miss this opportunity. Don't give in to pressure tactics. Remember, the "opportunity" is a chance to pay for information you could find yourself for free. Instead, visit the U.S. Department of Education's website studentaid.gov to find financial aid information.

 We guarantee you'll get aid. A company could claim it fulfilled its promise if you were offered student loans or a $200 scholarship. Is that worth a fee of $1,000 or more?

 I've got aid for you; give me your credit card or bank account number. Never give out a credit card or bank account number unless you know the organization you are giving it to is legitimate. You could be putting yourself at risk for identity theft.

---

[2] https://studentaid.gov/resources/scams

You Don't Have to Pay for the FAFSA Form

Several websites offer help filing the Free Application for Federal Student Aid (FAFSA) form for a fee. These sites are not affiliated with or endorsed by the U.S. Department of Education. The DOE urges you not to pay these sites for assistance that you can get for free elsewhere. The official FAFSA form is at fafsa.gov, and you can get free help from:

- the financial aid office at your college or the college(s) you're thinking about attending;

- the FAFSA form's online help at fafsa.gov; and

- the Federal Student Aid Information Center.

If you are asked for your credit card information while filling out the FAFSA form online, you are not at the official government site. Remember, the FAFSA site address has **.gov** in it.

You Don't Have to Pay for Help With Your Student Loans

Many student loan debt relief companies charge a fee to provide services that you can take care of yourself for free by contacting your loan servicer.

You can do any of the following for free:

- Lower or cap your monthly loan payment;

- Consolidate multiple federal student loans;

- Postpone monthly payments while you're furthering your education or are unemployed;

- Change your repayment plan; or

- See if you qualify for loan forgiveness.

Protect Your Personal Data

Criminals access personal data such as names, Social Security numbers, and bank and credit card information. Using the stolen data, the criminal can illegally obtain credit cards, set up cellphone accounts, and more.

How to Reduce Your Risk When Applying for Aid

- Apply for federal student aid by filling out the FAFSA form only at fafsa.gov.

- After completing the FAFSA form online, exit the application and close the browser; any cookies created during your session will be deleted automatically.

- Don't tell anyone your FSA ID, even if that person is helping you fill out the FAFSA form.

- Review your financial aid award documents and keep track of the amounts you applied for and received.

- Never give personal information over the phone or internet unless you made the contact. If you have questions about an offer of aid or about your student loan account, ask your college or contact the Federal Student Aid Information Center at 1-800-4FED-AID.

- When you complete a FAFSA application, your information is securely stored within the National Student Loan Data System (NSLDS) database and you can access it by visiting https://studentaid.ed.gov/log-in However, if you complete or even request a student loan application from a lender, you may be granting the lender permission to access your file. Before providing personal information to an organization, review its privacy policy.

- Keep receipts and documents (for example, credit applications or offers, checks and bank statements) with personal information in a safe place, and shred them when you are finished with them.

- Keep your purse or wallet safe at all times; store it and other items containing personal information in a secure place at home, especially if you have roommates.

- Immediately report all lost or stolen identification to the issuer (e.g., the credit card company or your state's Department of Motor Vehicles) and to the police, if appropriate.

The information you share with the Office of Federal Student Aid is kept safe via their secure websites (such as fafsa.gov and StudentLoans.gov). Data goes through a process called encryption. Encryption uses a mathematical formula to scramble your data into a format that is unreadable to a hacker.

Part 3: Paying Back Student Loans

Payment Details

Your lender or loan servicer must provide you with information about paying your loans. This includes your payment schedule, when you must begin paying, how many payments you must make to pay off the debt, and the amount of your payments.

The lender or servicer must also inform you about your **grace period**. This is the time between when you graduate, leave school, or change your status to part-time and when you must begin repaying your loan.

Some situations, such as a return to school or call to active military duty, may affect your grace period.

Direct subsidized loans, direct unsubsidized loans, subsidized federal Stafford loans, and unsubsidized federal Stafford loans have a six-month grace period. You must begin repaying PLUS loans when they are fully disbursed.

Be sure you know who your lenders are. Loans may be transferred to new loan servicers, for example. You should be notified of any changes, but if not, contact the original provider.

You can visit studentaid.gov to check the status of your financial aid and studentaid.gov/h/manage-loans for federal student loan payment information and to identify your loan servicer.

Federal student loans are assigned to loan servicers. These servicers provide assistance to clients for free. Some companies may offer to help you for a fee, but you should not need to pay anyone for help with federal student loans. Find contact information for your servicer through the Department of Education (studentaid.gov/manage-loans/repayment/servicers).

★ If you sign up for automatic monthly payments of federal student loans, you may get an interest rate reduction upon enrollment.

Loan Servicers

If you are still a student, contact your school's financial aid office for information about your loans.

Let your loan service provider know about any changes in your status, such as:

- Change of address
- Graduation
- Change to part-time enrollment

LOAN SERVICERS

The following are loan servicers for loans that the U.S. Department of Education owns.

Aidvantage
1-800-722-1300
aidvantage.com

HESC/Edfinancial
1-855-337-6884
www.edfinancial.com/DL

Default Resolution Group
1-800-621-3115
https://myeddebt.ed.gov

MOHELA
1-888-866-4352
www.mohela.com

ECSI
1-866-313-3797
https://efpls.ed.gov

Nelnet
1-888-486-4722
www.nelnet.com

FedLoan Servicing (PHEAA)
1-800-699-2908
www.myfedloan.org

OSLA Servicing
1-866-264-9762
www.osla.org

Great Lakes Educational Loan Services, Inc.
1-800-236-4300
www.mygreatlakes.org

Student Loan Forbearance Due to the Coronavirus Pandemic

On March 27, 2020, the CARES Act was signed into law. Part of that law provided broad relief for federal student loan borrowers. The CARES Act suspended federal student loan payments and provided for a temporary 0% interest rate on loans owned by the U.S. Department of Education until September 30, 2020. The suspension of federal student loan payments and the temporary 0% interest rate was extended several times after that. It was most recently extended until May 1, 2022.

Visit the Department of Education's website for more information about specific questions related to the Coronavirus pandemic as it relates to financial aid at https://studentaid.gov/announcements-events/covid-19

As borrowers are getting ready for student loan payments to resume on May 1, 2022, the Department of Education[3] recommends the following steps:

- Update your contact information in your profile on your loan servicer's website and in your StudentAid.gov profile.

- Review your auto-debit enrollment or sign up for the first time. To do so, log in to your loan servicer's website or contact your loan servicer directly.

- Check out their Loan Simulator at https://studentaid.gov/loan-simulator to find a repayment plan that meets your needs and goals or to decide whether to consolidate.

- Consider applying for an income-driven repayment (IDR) plan at https://studentaid.gov/app/ibrInstructions.action. An IDR plan can make your payments more affordable, depending on your income and family size.

Student Loan Assistance from Employers

A few companies help employees pay off student loans; it's called the Student Loan Repayment Benefit. This benefit is gaining popularity among U.S. companies. The Society for Human

---

[3] https://studentaid.gov/announcements-events/covid-19

Resource Management[4] reports that the number of companies who offer this benefit has doubled from 2018 to 2020, from 4% to 8%.

For the most part, companies that recruit and seek to retain young workers are more likely to offer this benefit. And, given the tight labor market in 2022, employers are looking for new ways to recruit young candidates. Be sure to ask about student loan repayment benefits when you are applying for a new job.

You should be able to get information about any student loan aid from your employer's human resources office.

Some companies offer a set annual reimbursement amount, while others reimburse employees for some student loan payments for a specific term. Some offer this benefit for only certain types of loans.

Be aware that student loan assistance is treated as taxable income. Be sure to understand any tax obligations you might have if you are offered this option.

---

[4]https://www.shrm.org/ResourcesAndTools/hr-topics/benefits/pages/shrm-benefits-survey-finds-renewed-focus-on-employee-wellbeing.aspx#loan-repayment

Here is a list of just some of the companies offering Student Loan Repayment Benefits.

EMPLOYERS OFFERING STUDENT LOAN ASSISTANCE

Company Name	Amount	Notes
Aetna	$2,000/yr	Full-time employees: matching contribution of $2,000/yr, up to $10,000
Ally Financial	$1,200/yr	Paid as $100/mo up to $10,000
Anderson Global	$1,200/yr	Paid as a lump sum based on $100/mo over 5 years, with an additional lump sum of $6,000
Carhartt	$600/yr	Paid as $50/mo up to $10,000
Carvana	$1,000/yr	For full-time employees only.
Chegg	$1,000/yr	Stock shares are also made available for student loan assistance.
Common Bond	$1,200/yr	$1,200 per year until the loan is paid off
Estee Lauder	$1,200/yr	Paid as $100/mo up to $10,000
Fidelity Investments		$15,000 maximum
First Republic Bank	$1,200 - $2,400/yr	Paid as $100/mo with increases to $200/mo
Google	$2,500/yr	Company will match up to $2,500 per year
Hulu	$1,200/yr	Paid as $100/mo up to $6,000

Company Name	Amount	Notes
LiveNation	$1,200/yr	Paid as $100/mo up to $6,000
Lockheed Martin	$1,800/yr	Paid as $150/mo up to $9,000
Natixis Global Asset Management	$1,000/yr	$1,000 per year and up to $10,000 over 10 years
New York Life	$2,040/yr	Paid as $170/mo up to $10,200 over 5 years
Nvidia	$6,000/yr	For recent graduates (in the last three years): Paid as $500/mo, up to $30,000
Peloton	$1,200/yr	Paid as $100/mo with no maximum
Penguin Random House	$1,200/yr	$1,200 per year and up to $9,000 over 7.5 years
Pepper Construction	$600/yr	Paid as $100/mo with no maximum
Price Waterhouse Coopers (PwC)	$1,200/yr	Paid as $100/mo for up to 6 years
SoFi	$2,400/yr	Paid as $200/mo
Staples	$1,200/yr	Paid as $100/mo up to $3,600 over 3 years
Terminix	$600/yr	Paid as $50/mo with no maximum

Sources:
https://www.nerdwallet.com/article/loans/student-loans/employer-student-loan-repayment
https://www.forbes.com/advisor/student-loans/companies-that-pay-student-loans/

Loan Consolidation

Some private lenders will let you consolidate your loans. This means that you can bundle your existing loans into a new loan with a new lender. You agree to pay the new lender the principal, which is the sum of your existing loans, plus interest, which is subject to a new interest rate. Your new lender will pay off your old student loans, so you only have to pay your new loan.

This may offer a number of advantages if you have private student loans. You may be able to get a new loan with a lower interest rate, and you can eliminate the chore of making monthly payments to several different lenders.

 Be cautious about refinancing federal student loans with a private lender.

If you refinance federal student loans with a private lender, you are likely to lose many of the benefits that make federal education loans valuable, such as deferment, forbearance, and forgiveness for working in public service.

A private lender may also charge you fees for consolidating loans. A lender could charge you a prepayment penalty—meaning you would pay a penalty for paying off your loans

early—while federal student loans have no prepayment penalty.

Federal student loans usually have the lowest interest rates, although if you have a great credit score you might be offered a lower rate through a private lender.

You may also choose another type of loan, such as a personal loan or home equity loan, in some situations.

Be sure you understand the terms and limitations of any consolidation. Calculate the cost and risk of any changes you make.

Repayment Plans

If you have student loan debt, and you want to pay it off, you have options on how much you will pay and how long you will have that debt. You can also make changes to your repayment plan if your life situation changes.

One option that holds appeal for many people early in their working life is an **income-driven repayment plan**. This means that your payments are based on how much you are earning now. If you consolidate your loans into a Direct Consolidation Loan, you may apply for the Revised Pay as You Earn Repayment Plan (REPAYE), Pay as You Earn Repayment Plan (PAYE), or Income-Contingent Repayment Plan (ICR).

You will need to complete the Income-Driven Repayment Plan Request, available from your loan servicer or through StudentLoans.gov. You may compare your payments using the Repayment Estimator at: https://studentaid.gov/loan-simulator/.

Under income-driven repayment plans, monthly payment amounts are determined by the plan you choose. Generally, these are:

- **REPAYE Plan**: 10 percent of your discretionary income.

- **PAYE Plan**: 10 percent of your discretionary income, but no more than the amount you would pay under the ten-year Standard Repayment Plan.

- **IBR Plan**: 10 percent of your discretionary income for new borrowers on or after July 1, 2014. If you are not a new borrower on or after July 1, 2014, usually 15 percent of your discretionary income. In either case, no more than the amount you would pay under the ten-year Standard Repayment Plan.

- **ICR Plan**: Whichever is less: 20 percent of your discretionary

income, or the amount you would pay over twelve years on a fixed-income repayment plan (adjusted for income).

Other repayment options include **standard and graduated plans**. Both types are for ten-year terms. A person earning $25,000 a year initially, enrolled in the standard repayment plan with initial debt of $30,000 in direct unsubsidized loans, would pay $333 monthly for a total of $39,967 after ten years. With a graduated repayment plan, payment might start at $190 a month, but gradually increase to as high as $571, for a total of $42,636.

Take a look at the chart on the next page to compare what you would pay under each of the repayment plans.

If you choose a standard plan, your monthly payments will be the same for ten years. The higher payments may be difficult for people just beginning their careers, but under the standard and graduated plans, the debt will be paid off in half the time of the income-based payment plans.

If you enroll in an income-based repayment plan, you do not have to stay in it for the full term. You can change your plan to increase payments and reduce the amount of interest you will pay. You can also pay more, to pay your loan off more quickly as you earn more money.

REPAYING A $30,000 LOAN

Undergraduate loan debt of $30,000 in direct unsubsidized loans, starting income $25,000

Plan	Initial Payment	Final Payment	Time in Repayment	Total Paid
Standard	$333	$333	10 years	$39,967
Graduated	$190	$571	10 years	$42,636
REPAYE	$60	$296	20 years	$32,358
PAYE & IBR (new borrower)	$60	$296	20 years	$39,517
IBR (not new borrower)	$90	$333	21 years, 10 months	$61,006
ICR	$195	$253	19 years, 6 months	$52,233

Some private lenders also offer a variety of payment plans, including income-based plans. Discuss your situation with the lender and find out if you can change your payment plan to best suit your needs, and what your options are if your financial situation changes.

You may also be able to find options to pay loans off over very long time periods. The idea of making smaller payments can be appealing, but the long-term consequences can be expensive.

Your debt will continue to grow as the interest adds up. Usually, the best idea is to pay debt off quickly. If you start off with a long-term loan, try to switch to a plan that will allow you to pay off the loans more quickly if your situation changes and you can afford larger payments. If you get a raise, a better job, or reduce your expenses, reevaluate your monthly student loan payments and see if you can pay the debt down.

Medical & Healthcare Field

If you are studying to be a medical professional, you may be eligible for a health professions student loan. These loans are for future dentists, doctors, nurses, pharmacists, and veterinarians, for example. You can learn more from the US Department of Health and Human Services at: https://bhw.hrsa.gov/loans-scholarships.

 Loan Forgiveness, Cancellation, or Discharge

If you work in certain professions, some or all of your federal student loans may be forgiven. These include public service careers, including education, government, nonprofits, medicine, and volunteer organizations such as the Peace Corps.

The financial aid staff at your school will tell you about any loan forgiveness programs related to your field of study.

The National Health Service Corps at https://nhsc.hrsa.gov/loan-repayment/index.html pays up to $50,000 toward student loans for eligible employees working at approved sites, while medical or dental students may be eligible for the Students to Service Loan Repayment Program. Health professionals providing primary care may qualify for the State Loan Repayment Program.

If you are working as a nurse, you can apply for the Nurse Corps Loan Repayment Program at https://bhw.hrsa.gov/loans-scholarships/nurse-corps/loan-repayment-program.

Federal student loans may be forgiven, cancelled, or discharged under certain circumstances. Discuss your situation with your loan servicers to determine if you are eligible and how much you qualify for. A number of programs are available, but with different requirements.

Closed School Discharge

If the school you are attending closes, or it closes within 120 days after you withdraw, you may be eligible to have your loans discharged. That means you may no longer be obligated to pay them.

You must apply for the discharge through your loan servicer, and you must continue to make payments during the discharge process. If you have completed your program of study, you are not eligible for discharge, even if the school then closes. If your application is approved, you may be eligible for a refund of payments you have made. The discharge should also be reported to credit agencies, and any negative events related to the loan should be deleted. If your discharge is denied, you may be able to apply to recover some of the tuition through your state education licensing agency. If the school filed for bankruptcy, you can file a claim in the court system. You may need a lawyer to assist you.

Public Service Loan Forgiveness (PSLF)

This program forgives your remaining balance on *direct loans* once you have made 120 qualifying monthly payments under a qualifying repayment plan while a full-time employee of a qualifying employer.

Qualifying employers are government organizations, tax-exempt 501(c)(3) not-for profit organizations, and some other not-for-profit organizations that provide some public services. Full-

time AmeriCorps or Peace Corps work also counts.

Time spent in religious instruction, worship services, and similar activities may not count as work hours. If you simultaneously hold more than one qualifying part-time job for a combined average of thirty hours a week or more, this counts as full-time.

Loans from federal student loan programs other than the William D. Ford Federal Direct Loan Program may be eligible if you consolidate them. If you do so, your previous payments do not count toward the 120 qualifying payments.

You cannot get credit for making extra payments or larger payments than required. Qualifying payments include income-driven repayment plans and the ten-year standard repayment plan; with the latter, however, your loan should be paid off after 120 payments, so you should contact your loan servicer to change to an income-driven repayment plan if you wish to pursue loan forgiveness.

While working to meet PSLF requirements, complete the Employment Certification for Public Service Loan Forgiveness form (https://studentaid.ed.gov/sa/sites/.../ public-service-application-for-forgiveness.pdf) annually or when you change jobs, and submit it to be sure you are meeting the requirements.

When you have made your 120 qualifying payments, you may apply for loan forgiveness. Contact your loan servicer for information.

★ The U.S. Department of Education changed the Public Service Loan Forgiveness program rules in October 2021. For a limited period of time, through October 21, 2022, borrowers may receive credit for past periods of repayment that would otherwise not qualify for the PSLF program.

If you wish to apply for public service loan forgiveness for federal loans, visit https://studentaid.gov/manage-loans/forgiveness-cancellation/public-service

Teacher Loan Forgiveness

If you work for five full, consecutive academic years in some schools and agencies (since 2004), you may be eligible for forgiveness of up to $17,500 on direct subsidized and unsubsidized loans and subsidized and unsubsidized Federal Stafford

Loans. You must not be in default at any time, and teaching through AmeriCorps will not count. Qualifying schools are generally low-income schools—you can search the list of schools at: https://studentaid.gov/app/tcliDirectorySearch.action Also included are elementary and secondary schools operated by or under contract with the Bureau of Indian Education (BIE).

Highly-qualified elementary and secondary school teachers may receive up to $5,000 loan forgiveness, while highly-qualified secondary school full-time mathematics and science teachers and highly qualified special education teachers who primarily offered special education to children with disabilities may receive up to $17,500 in loan forgiveness.

You will need to complete the Teacher Loan Forgiveness Application at: (https://studentaid.gov/app/downloadForm.action?searchType=library&shortName=teachfrgv&localeCode=en-us) and submit it to your loan holder or servicer. If you have loans with different loan holders or servicers, you must submit forms to each.

Perkins Loan Cancellation and Discharge

Under federal law, the authority for schools to make new Perkins Loans ended on Sept. 30, 2017, and final disbursements were permitted through June 30, 2018. As a result, students can no longer receive Perkins Loans.

If you had a Federal Perkins Loan, you may be eligible for loan cancellation if you have served in an area of hostilities with the U.S. armed forces, volunteered in the Peace Corps or ACTION program, or worked as a nurse or medical technician, in law enforcement/corrections, Head Start, child or family services, are a professional in early intervention services, or worked as a teacher.

Contact the school that made the loan for information about deferment and cancellation. Teachers must be employed full-time for a full academic year (or two consecutive half-years) in a qualifying position at a qualifying low-income school or BIE-owned or – operated school. You may be eligible if you teach part-time in two or more schools. You may also qualify if you provide special education services such as recreational therapy and speech and language pathology, or teach a subject for which teachers are in short supply in your state. You may also qualify if you teach languages, math, and sciences.

You may be eligible for cancellation of 15 percent of your Perkins loan for the first and second years of service, 20 percent for the third and fourth years, and 30 percent for the fifth year (including the accrued interest that year).

Total and Permanent Disability Discharge

If you become totally and permanently disabled, you may qualify for discharge of direct loans, Federal Family Education Loans, and Federal Perkins Loans. You may also complete a Teacher Education Assistance for College and Higher Education (TEACH) Grant service obligation. You must complete a discharge application, including appropriate documentation of your claim of disability, and send it to the Nelnet Total and Permanent Disability Servicer. Depending on your circumstances, you could be entitled to have loan payments you made after the date of disability returned. For more information and an application, visit: disabilitydischarge.com.

Discharge Due to Death

Federal student loans may be discharged following the death of the borrower or of the student for whom a PLUS loan was taken. A family member or representative must provide qualifying proof of death, such as a death certificate, to the loan servicer.

Discharge in Bankruptcy (in rare cases)

If you wish to have your federal student loan discharged in bankruptcy, you must ask the bankruptcy court to decide that making the loan payments presents an undue hardship on you and your dependents. This action is called an adversary proceeding. Discharge is possible under Chapter 7 or Chapter 13 bankruptcy. The bankruptcy court could decide to fully discharge your loan (you owe nothing more), partially discharge it (leaving you with a portion to repay), or set new terms for full repayment (such as a lower interest rate). Parents may also seek discharge of PLUS loans in bankruptcy.

False Certification of Student Eligibility or Unauthorized Payment Discharge

You may be able to have a Direct Loan discharged due to false certification[5]:

- The school falsely certified your eligibility to receive the loan based on your ability to benefit from its training, and you didn't

meet the ability-to-benefit student eligibility requirements.

- The school certified your eligibility to receive the loan, but at the time of the certification, you had a status (physical or mental condition, age, criminal record, or other circumstance) that disqualified you from meeting the legal requirements for employment in your state of residence in the occupation for which the program of study was preparing you.

- The school signed your name on the loan application or promissory note without your authorization or the school endorsed your loan check or signed your authorization for electronic funds transfer without your knowledge, and the loan money wasn't given to you or applied to charges you owed to the school.

Visit https://studentaid.gov/manage-loans/forgiveness-cancellation/false-certification for specific information about discharge eligibility.

Unpaid Refund Discharge

You may be eligible for discharge of the unpaid refund of a Direct Loan or FFEL Program loan if you withdrew from school but the school issued a refund to the lender or U.S.

---

[5] https://studentaid.gov/manage-loans/forgiveness-cancellation/false-certification

Department of Education. Contact the school and the loan servicer for information.

Borrower Defense Discharge

If the school misled you or violated some laws, you may be eligible for forgiveness of student loans. You must complete an application, available at: https://studentaid.gov/manage-loans/forgiveness-cancellation/borrower-defense. You may be required to include transcripts to prove enrollment, correspondence with school officials, and materials such as course catalogues from the school.

If you are eligible, you may have all or part of your federal student loans forgiven, and may be entitled to repayment of the amount you have already paid on loans. While your application is being considered, you may have all federal student loans on which you are paying placed into forbearance. Although you are temporarily not required to make payments, the loan will continue to accrue interest, and you may make payments if you wish. You may also achieve stopped-collections status, which means debt collection companies will not try to collect on the loan during this time, and your wages and income tax refunds will not be withheld to pay creditors.

If your application is accepted, some or all of your federal student loans will be discharged. Forbearance and/or stopped-collections periods end when the application is accepted or denied.

Ways to Avoid Student Debt in the First Place

Keeping your student loan debt down to a minimum is an important step to paying down your student loans. The less you have to pay back means more money in your pocket after graduation.

Grants

Apply for grants! Most grants do not need to be paid back and can go a long way in reducing your student loan debt. Each year, billions of dollars in grants go unused, so make sure you take the time to apply.

Scholarships & Awards

Take the time to research and apply for scholarships, which do not need to be paid back. There may be scholarships or awards available from local community organizations, within specific areas of interest or for a specific career path.

Employer Tuition Reimbursement

Many employers offer tuition reimbursement for both undergraduate and master's degrees.

Explore Schools with Lower Tuition Costs

You could potentially save thousands over the course of your degree by attending a college in-state, choosing a school that has lower tuition costs, or pursuing a career path that has extra scholarships or awards.

Get College Credit in High School

You can reduce the number of classes you need to take in college by enrolling in Advanced Placement (AP) or International Baccalaureate (IB) courses. These courses can be used for college credit.

Make Each Semester Count

Most colleges charge the same amount if you take three or six courses per semester. You may be able to save the cost of a full semester, just by taking the maximum number of courses each semester. Check with your institution about their requirements.

Education Benefits for the Military

Active military members can take advantage of tuition assistance and education benefits.

An application to apply for GI Bill Education Benefits can be downloaded here: http://www.vba.va.gov/pubs/forms/VBA-22-1990-ARE.pdf

Montgomery GI Bill (Active Duty)

The Montgomery GI Bill (MGIB) is an educational assistance program that provides up to 36 months of education benefits to those who have served on active duty.

Assistance may be used for college degree and certificate programs, technical or vocational courses, flight training, apprenticeships or on-the-job training, high-tech training, licensing and certification tests, entrepreneurship training, certain entrance examinations, and correspondence courses.

Military members may be an eligible if they have an honorable discharge; AND have a high school diploma or GED or in some cases 12 hours of college credit; AND meet additional requirements listed on the VA's website:

https://www.va.gov/education/about-gi-bill-benefits/montgomery-active-duty/

Montgomery GI Bill (Selected Reserve)

The MGIB-Selected Reserve program provides up to 36 months of education benefits to eligible members of the Selected Reserve. To be eligible, candidates must: incur a six-year obligation to serve in the Selected Reserve after June 30, 1985; complete their Initial Active Duty for Training (IADT); remain in good standing while serving in an active Selected Reserve unit; and complete high school or have a high school equivalency certificate.

Post 9/11 GI Bill

The Post 9/11 GI Bill is an educational assistance program enacted by Congress for individuals with active duty service after September 10, 2001. The Post-9/11 GI Bill provides up to 36 months of education benefits.

To qualify, service members must have served: 90 days of active duty service after September 10, 2001; OR 30 continuous days after September 10, 2001, and be discharged due to a service-connected disability.

If you are a military service member and have questions about education assistance, visit

https://gibill.custhelp.va.gov/ to search Frequently Asked Questions or ask a question electronically, or call (888) 442-4551.

Tactics for Paying Off Loan Debt

Put together a budget that shows how much you earn and how much you owe each month. Start by tracking every penny for a month. This will show you exactly how much you spend and what you have left over after paying the necessary bills. You may find areas that you can cut back on, such as unnecessary clothing purchases, and use this money to pay off student loans and other debt. You can use the Budget Worksheet on page 46 to get started, or you can search online for a budget calculator and other money management tools.

You may be able to make payments even while you are in school. Ask your loan servicer if you can pay interest or principal (your loan amount) before you graduate.

Put extra money toward paying loans when you can. This reduces the interest you will pay, and in the end the total amount you pay will be lower. Make sure you tell your loan servicer that extra payments are not to be used for future payments, but should be applied immediately.

Pay toward the loan with the highest interest rate first. This strategy of tackling the debt with the highest interest rate first is called *debt stacking* or a *debt avalanche*. It saves you the most money on interest. You can even set up automatic monthly payments to include extra money toward your loan debt. This makes it more difficult to change your mind if you're tempted to spend that money somewhere else. If you reduce expenses or earn more money, increase your monthly payments toward debt.

The opposite of a debt avalanche is a *debt snowball*. With this strategy, you work hardest to pay off the smallest debt, then move up the line. This is not the best strategy for paying off debt, because it does not tackle interest, but it may motivate you to keep working by eliminating bills.

Make an extra payment every year, painlessly; instead of making your monthly payment every four weeks, split it in half and pay every two weeks. At the end of the year (fifty-two weeks), you will have made thirteen monthly payments. Set up automatic payment through your bank to make it more convenient. This is an especially good method if you are paid every two weeks, because it affects all paychecks equally.

Consolidate some or all of your federal student loans, if possible, to get a lower interest rate. Evaluate your potential to pay off loans early, however, because if you consolidate all of your loans, you will not be able to pay off high-interest loans first. A loan consolidation and debt payoff calculator can help you see how much you can accomplish through these actions, and offer some incentive. Consolidated loan repayment plans may range from seven to thirty years. You can use FinAid's debt consolidation calculator here, to see if you can save: https://finaid.org/calculators/loancons olidation/

Use extra funds to pay off debt. These may include part or all of any gifts, bonuses, raises, or tax refunds you receive. The long-term benefit is more useful to your financial well-being than a short-term splurge. See accelerated debt payoff calculator at: https://finaid.org/calculators/prepaym ent/ to calculate how much you can save and how quickly you can pay off the debt.

Interest paid on student loans is usually tax deductible. Your annual deduction is limited and is only for loans used for school expenses, including tuition and room and board. You may also earn a tax credit for having student loans. The American Opportunity credit is available to students making tuition payments, including funds from student loans. The Lifetime Learning credit is for students who have completed four years of education. It covers tuition and fees, including those paid using student loans. Tax law may change, so consult a tax preparer or use tax software that helps you make the most of such tax credits.

Emergency Measures

Contact your loan servicer immediately if you are having financial problems. Do not wait until you have missed one or more payments. Missing or late payments will affect your credit score. In many cases even bankruptcy will not erase student loan debt.

Consider loan deferment or forbearance only after you have exhausted other options, such as switching to an income-driven repayment plan. For example, a single person making less than $1,486 a month on an income-driven repayment plan may have a monthly payment of $0. This alleviates the pressure and puts a payment plan into place. Deferment and forbearance, on the other hand, will usually increase your debt because interest will continue to accrue.

Deferment allows you to temporarily delay making payments on the principal and interest. In some cases the federal government will pay the interest on subsidized loans or Perkins loans during this time. Interest will still add up, and increase your overall debt.

You may qualify for deferment if you:

- are unemployed or unable to find full-time employment;

- are called to active military service;

- attend school part-time;

- are enrolled in an approved graduate fellowship program or rehabilitation training program;

- are experiencing economic hardship; or

- performing some services (or in some cases for up to thirteen months) following active-duty military service.

Contact your loan servicer to discuss your situation and determine eligibility.

Forbearance may allow you to stop making payments, or reduce payments, for up to a year. Your lender decides if you qualify for discretionary forbearance due to financial hardship or illness. You may ask for mandatory forbearance if:

- your monthly student loan payment is 20 percent or more of your total monthly gross income;

- you are seeking teacher loan forgiveness or repayment under the U.S. Department of Defense Student Loan Repayment Program;

- you are serving in a dental or medical residency program;

- are serving in a national service position for which you have received a national service award; or

- you have been activated by a governor in your role with the National Guard.

Your loans will continue to accrue interest, which you may choose to pay during forbearance. Contact your servicer to request forbearance and discuss terms.

Financial Strategies

You can find ways to reduce your expenses and pay debt more quickly. This does not mean you must live without streaming services or fine dining forever. By increasing your student loan payments for a few years, you can pay off a lot of debt. Even a few months of frugal living can make a dent in your debt.

Take it one month at a time—buy only essentials for four weeks, and see how much you can save. If you do this even a few times a year, and use that money to pay off some debt, you will see a difference.

To explore ways to evaluate and potentially reduce your living expenses take a look at, *How to Manage Debt*, another guide in this series.

Appendices

Budget Worksheet

Month/Year: _____

Monthly Income

Wages	_____
Tips	_____
Other Income	_____
TOTAL MONTHLY INCOME	_____

Monthly Expenses

HOUSING	Mortgage/Rent	_____
	Utilities (Electricity/Water)	_____
	Credit Cards	_____
	Insurance (Homeowners, Renters, etc.)	_____
	Loan Payments	_____
	Other Housing Expenses (Cable, Internet, etc.)	_____
FOOD	Groceries/Household Supplies	_____
	Restaurant and Other Food	_____
TRANSPORTATION	Public Transportation	_____
	Vehicle Loan	_____
	Gas for Personal Vehicle	_____
	Parking, Tolls, etc.	_____
	Maintenance & Supplies (oil, etc.)	_____
	Vehicle Insurance	_____
HEALTH	Health Insurance	_____
	Medicine/Prescriptions	_____
	Other (Dental, Vision, Copays)	_____
PERSONAL	Childcare or Support	_____
	Other Family Support	_____
	Laundry	_____
	Clothing, Shoes, etc.	_____
	Charitable Gifts, Donations, etc.	_____
	Entertainment (Movies, etc.)	_____
	Other (Haircuts, etc.)	_____
DEBT & FINANCE	Debt (Credit Cards, etc.)	_____
	Student Loans or Other Debts	_____
	Fees (Bank, Credit Card, Debit)	_____
	Prepaid Cards, Phone Cards, etc.	_____
MISCELLANEOUS EXPENSES	Supplies (School, etc.)	_____
	Pet Care	_____
	Other	_____
	TOTAL MONTHLY EXPENSES	_____

TOTAL MONTHLY INCOME	_____
subtract your **TOTAL MONTHLY EXPENSES**	_____
=	_____

Banks and Consolidation Rates

	Variable Rates	Loan Types	Terms (in years)
CommonBond	2.50% - 6.85%	Variable & Fixed	5, 7, 10, 15, 20
Earnest	1.99% - 5.89%	Variable & Fixed	5 to 20
Education Loan Finance	1.86% - 6.01%	Variable & Fixed	5, 7, 10, 15, 20
LendKey	1.90% - 5.25%	Variable & Fixed	5, 7, 10, 15, 20
Navient Refinancing	1.74% - 5.64%	Variable & Fixed	5 to 20
PenFed Credit Union	2.13% - 5.25%	Variable & Fixed	5, 8, 12, 15
SoFi	1.74% - 7.24%	Variable & Fixed	5, 7, 10, 15, 20
Splash Financial	1.74% - 7.49%	Variable & Fixed	5 to 25

This information is subject to change. Consult your loan provider for specific information about consolidation terms and rates.

Source: https://studentloanhero.com/featured/5-banks-to-refinance-your-student-loans/

Where to Find Financial Aid, Grants & Scholarships

Federal
US Department of Education, Federal Student Aid
https://studentaid.gov

Alabama
Alabama Commission on Higher Education
https://ache.edu/

Alaska
Alaska Commission on Postsecondary Education
https://acpesecure.alaska.gov/

Arizona
Arizona Commission for Postsecondary Education
https://azgrants.az.gov/available-grants

Arkansas
Arkansas Department of Higher Education
https://scholarships.adhe.edu/

California
California Student Aid Commission
https://www.csac.ca.gov/financial-aid-programs

Colorado
Colorado Department of Higher Education
https://highered.colorado.gov/students/preparing-for-college/financial-aid-for-
students

Connecticut
Connecticut Office of Higher Education
https://www.ctohe.org/SFA/default.shtml

Delaware
Delaware Department of Education
https://delawarestudentsuccess.org/resources/fund-your-education/

District Columbia
DC Office of the State Superintendent of Education
https://osse.dc.gov/dctag

Florida
Florida Department of Education, Office of Student Financial Assistance
https://www.floridastudentfinancialaidsg.org/SAPHome/SAPHome?url=home

Georgia
Georgia Student Finance Commission
https://www.gafutures.org/hope-state-aid-programs/

Hawaii
Hawaii State Department of Education
https://www.hawaiipublicschools.org/lists/scholarships/allitems.aspx

Idaho
Idaho State Board of Education
https://boardofed.idaho.gov/scholarships/

Illinois
Illinois Student Assistance Commission
https://www.isac.org/

Indiana
Indiana Commission for Higher Education
https://www.in.gov/che/

Iowa
Iowa College Student Aid Commission
https://www.iowacollegeaid.gov/ScholarshipsAndGrants

Kansas
Kansas Board of Regents
https://www.kansasregents.org/scholarships_and_grants

Kentucky
Kentucky Higher Education Assistance Authority
https://www.kheaa.com/website/kheaa/kheaaprograms?main=1

Louisiana
Louisiana Office of Student Financial Assistance
https://mylosfa.la.gov/students-parents/scholarships-grants/

Maine
Finance Authority of Maine
https://www.famemaine.com/affording-education/pay-for-school/maine-grant-
         tuition-programs/

Maryland
Maryland Higher Education Commission
https://mhec.maryland.gov/preparing/Pages/FinancialAid/index.aspx

Massachusetts
Massachusetts Department of Higher Education
https://www.mass.edu/osfa/home/home.asp

Michigan
Michigan Student Financial Services Bureau
https://www.michigan.gov/mistudentaid

Minnesota
Minnesota Office of Higher Education
https://www.ohe.state.mn.us/

Mississippi
MS Institutions of Higher Learning
https://www.msfinancialaid.org/

Missouri

Missouri Department of Higher Education
https://dhewd.mo.gov/ppc/grants/

Montana

Montana Higher Education Student Assistance Program
https://www.reachhighermontana.org/

Nebraska

Coordinating Commission for Postsecondary Education
https://ccpe.nebraska.gov/nebraska-opportunity-grant-nog

Nevada

Nevada State Treasurer
https://www.nevadatreasurer.gov/GGMS/GGMS_Home/

New Hampshire

New Hampshire Department of Education
https://www.nhheaf.org/

New Jersey

New Jersey Higher Education Student Assistance Authority
https://www.hesaa.org/Pages/NJGrantsHome.aspx

New Mexico

New Mexico Higher Education Department
https://hed.state.nm.us/students-parents

New York

New York Higher Education Services Corporation
https://www.hesc.ny.gov/pay-for-college/apply-for-financial-aid/apply-for-aid-start-
here.html

North Carolina

College Foundation of North Carolina
https://www.cfnc.org/pay-for-college/apply-for-financial-aid/nc-community-
college-grant/

North Dakota
North Dakota University System
https://ndus.edu/paying-for-college/

Ohio
Ohio Department of Higher Education
https://www.ohiohighered.org/sgs

Oklahoma
Oklahoma College Assistance Program
https://secure.okcollegestart.org/Financial_Aid_Planning/Scholarships/_default.aspx

Oregon
Oregon Higher Education Coordinating Commission
https://oregonstudentaid.gov/

Pennsylvania
Pennsylvania Higher Education Assistance Agency
https://www.pheaa.org/

Rhode Island
Rhode Island Student Loan Authority
https://www.rischolarships.org/

South Carolina
South Carolina Commission on Higher Education
https://www.che.sc.gov/InstitutionsEducators.aspx#ScholarshipGrantInfo

South Dakota
South Dakota Board of Regents
https://www.sdbor.edu/student-information/Pages/Paying-for-College.aspx

Tennessee
Tennessee Student Assistance Corporation
https://www.tn.gov/collegepays/financial-aid.html

Texas

Texas Higher Education Coordinating Board
https://www.highered.texas.gov/

Utah

Utah System of Higher Education
https://ushe.edu/initiatives/state-aid-programs/

Vermont

Vermont Student Assistance Corporation
https://www.vsac.org/

Virginia

State Council of Higher Education for Virginia
https://www.schev.edu/

Washington

Washington Student Achievement Council
https://wsac.wa.gov/financial-aid

West Virginia

College Foundation of West Virginia
https://secure.cfwv.com/Financial_Aid_Planning/Scholarships/Scholarships.aspx

Wisconsin

State of Wisconsin Higher Educational Aids Board
https://heab.state.wi.us/programs.html

Wyoming

Wyoming Department of Education
https://edu.wyoming.gov/for-parents-students/hathaway-scholarship-information/

Income-Driven Repayment Plans
& Direct Consolidation Loans

Apply for an Income Driven Repayment Plan

Visit https://studentaid.gov/app/ibrInstructions.action

This application can be used for Pay As You Earn (PAYE), Revised Pay As You Earn (REPAYE), Income-Based (IBR), or Income-Contingent (ICR) repayment.

Apply for a Complete Direct Consolidation Loan

Visit https://studentaid.gov/app/lcHtml.action

A Direct Consolidation Loan allows you to consolidate (combine) multiple federal education loans into one loan at no cost to you.

FAFSA®

FREE APPLICATION *for* FEDERAL STUDENT AID

July 1, 2022 – June 30, 2023

Federal Student Aid
An OFFICE of the U.S. DEPARTMENT of EDUCATION

PROUD SPONSOR *of*
the AMERICAN MIND®

Use this form to apply free for federal and state student grants, work-study, and loans.

Or apply free online at **fafsa.gov**.

Apply by the Deadlines

For federal aid, submit your application as early as possible, but no earlier than October 1, 2021. We must receive your application no later than June 30, 2023. Your college must have your correct, complete information by your last day of enrollment in the 2022-2023 school year.

For state or college aid, the deadline may be as early as October 2021. See the table to the right for state deadlines. You may also need to complete additional forms.

Check with your high school counselor or a financial aid administrator at your college about state and college sources of student aid and deadlines.

If you are filing close to one of these deadlines, we recommend you file either online at **fafsa.gov** or via the myStudentAid mobile app. These are the fastest and easiest ways to apply for aid.

Use Your Tax Return

We recommend that you complete and submit your FAFSA form as soon as possible on or after October 1, 2021. The easiest way to complete or correct your FAFSA form with accurate tax information is by using the IRS Data Retrieval Tool either through **fafsa.gov** or the myStudentAid mobile app. In a few simple steps, most students and parents who filed a 2020 tax return can transfer their tax return information directly into their FAFSA form.

If you (or your parents) have missed the 2020 tax filing deadline and still need to file a 2020 income tax return with the Internal Revenue Service (IRS), you should submit your FAFSA form now using estimated tax information, and then you **must correct** that information **after you file** your return.

Note: Both parents or both the student and spouse may need to report income information on the FAFSA form if they did not file a joint tax return for 2020. For assistance with answering the income information questions in this situation, call 1-800-4-FED-AID (1-800-433-3243).

Fill Out the FAFSA® Form

If you or your family experienced significant changes to your financial situation (such as loss of employment), or other unusual circumstances (such as tuition expenses at an elementary or secondary school or high unreimbursed medical or dental expenses), complete this form to the extent you can and submit it as instructed. Consult with the financial aid office at the college(s) you applied to or plan to attend.

For help in filling out the FAFSA form, go to **StudentAid.gov/completefafsa** or call 1-800-433-3243.

Fill the answer fields directly on your screen or print the form and complete it by hand. Your answers will be read electronically; therefore, if you complete the form by hand:

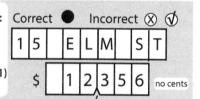

- use black ink and fill in circles completely:
- print clearly in CAPITAL letters and skip a box between words:
- report dollar amounts (such as $12,356.41) like this:

Blue is for student information and purple is for parent information.

Mail Your FAFSA® Form

After you complete this application, make a copy of pages 3 through 8 for your records. Then mail the original of pages 3 through 8 to:

Federal Student Aid Programs, P.O. Box 7650, London, KY 40742-7650.

After your application is processed, you will receive a summary of your information in your *Student Aid Report* (SAR). If you provide an e-mail address, your SAR will be sent by e-mail within three to five days. If you do not provide an e-mail address, your SAR will be mailed to you within three weeks. If you would like to check the status of your application, go to **fafsa.gov** or call 1-800-433-3243.

Let's Get Started!

Now go to page 3 of the FAFSA form and begin filling it out. Refer to the notes on pages 9 and 10 as instructed.

The Federal Student Aid logo and FAFSA are registered trademarks of Federal Student Aid, U.S. Department of Education.

Pay attention to any symbols listed after your state deadline.
States and territories not included in the main listing below: AL♦, AS♦*, AZ♦, CO♦, FM♦*, GU♦*, HI♦*, KY^$, MH♦*, NC^$, ND^$, NE♦, NH♦*, NM♦, OK^$, PR♦, PW♦*, RI♦*, SD♦*, UT♦$*, VA♦*, VI♦*, VT^$*, WA^♦, WI♦ and WY♦*.

State	Deadline
AK	Alaska Education Grant ^ $ Alaska Performance Scholarship: June 30, 2022 # $
AR	Academic Challenge: July 1, 2022 *(date received)* ArFuture Grant: fall term, July 1, 2022 *(date received)*; spring term, Jan. 10, 2023 *(date received)*
CA	For many state financial aid programs: March 2, 2022 *(date postmarked)*. Cal Grant also requires submission of a school-certified GPA by March 2, 2022. For additional community college Cal Grants: Sept. 2, 2022 *(date postmarked)*. For noncitizens without a Social Security card or with one issued through the federal Deferred Action for Childhood Arrivals (DACA) program, fill out the *California Dream Act Application*. Contact the California Student Aid Commission or your financial aid administrator for more information.
CT	Feb. 15, 2022 *(date received)* # ♦ *
DC	FAFSA form completed by Aug. 19, 2022 # For DC Tuition Assistance Grant, complete the DC OneApp and submit supporting documents by Aug. 26, 2022. #
DE	April 15, 2022 *(date received)*
FL	May 15, 2022 *(date processed)*
GA	Refer to Georgia Student Finance Commission's web site for additional information. ^♦ *
IA	July 1, 2022 *(date received)*; earlier priority deadlines may exist for certain programs. *
ID	Opportunity Scholarship: March 1, 2022 *(date received)* # ♦ *
IL	Refer to the Illinois Student Assistance Commission's web site for the Monetary Award Program (MAP) renewal deadline. ^ $
IN	Adult Student Grant ^ $: New applicants must submit additional form. Workforce Ready Grant ^ Frank O'Bannon Grant: April 15, 2022 *(date received)* 21st Century Scholarship: April 15, 2022 *(date received)*
KS	April 1, 2022 *(date received)* # ♦ *
LA	July 1, 2023 (Feb. 1, 2022, recommended)
MA	May 1, 2022 *(date received)* #
MD	March 1, 2022 *(date received)*
ME	May 1, 2022 *(date received)*
MI	March 1, 2022 *(date received)*
MN	30 days after term starts *(date received)*
MO	Feb. 1, 2022 # Applications accepted through April 1, 2022 *(date received)*
MP	April 30, 2022 *(date received)* # *
MS	MTAG and MESG Grants: Oct. 15, 2022 *(date received)* HELP Grant: April 30, 2022 *(date received)*
MT	Dec. 1, 2021 # ♦ *
NJ	Renewal applicants (2021–2022 Tuition Aid Grant recipients): April 15, 2022 *(date received)* All other applicants: fall and spring terms, Sept. 15, 2022 *(date received)*; spring term only, Feb. 15, 2023 *(date received)*
NV	Silver State Opportunity Grant ^ $ Nevada Promise Scholarship: March 1, 2022 * $ All other aid ♦ *
NY	June 30, 2023 *(date received)* *
OH	Oct. 1, 2022 *(date received)*
OR	Oregon Opportunity Grant ^ $ OSAC Private Scholarships: March 1, 2022 * Oregon Promise Grant: Contact state agency. *
PA	All first-time applicants enrolled in a community college; business/trade/technical school; hospital school of nursing; designated Pennsylvania open-admission institution; or nontransferable two-year program: Aug. 1, 2022 *(date received)* All other applicants: May 1, 2022 *(date received)* *
SC	SC Commission on Higher Education Need-based Grants ^ $ Tuition Grants: June 30, 2022 *(date received)*
TN	State Grant: Prior-year recipients receive award if eligible and apply by Feb. 1, 2022; all other awards made to neediest applicants. $ Tennessee Promise: Feb. 1, 2022 *(date received)* State Lottery: fall term, Sept. 1, 2022 *(date received)*; spring and summer terms, Feb. 1, 2023 *(date received)*
TX	Jan. 15, 2022 # * Private and two-year institutions may have different deadlines. ♦
WV	PROMISE Scholarship: March 1, 2022. New applicants must submit additional form. Contact your financial aid administrator or state agency. WV Higher Education Grant: April 15, 2022 WV Invests Grant: April 15, 2022 #

* Additional forms may be required.   ^ As soon as possible after Oct. 1, 2021.
♦ Check with your financial aid administrator.   # For priority consideration, submit by date specified.
$ Awards made until funds are depleted.

STATE AID DEADLINES

What is the FAFSA® form?

Why fill out a FAFSA form?

The *Free Application for Federal Student Aid* (FAFSA) is the first step in the financial aid process. You use the FAFSA form to apply for federal student aid, such as grants, work-study, and loans. In addition, most states and colleges use information from the FAFSA form to award nonfederal aid.

Why all the questions?

Most of the questions on the FAFSA form are required to calculate your Expected Family Contribution (EFC). The EFC measures your family's financial strength and is used to determine your eligibility for federal student aid. Your state and the colleges you list may also use some of your responses. They will determine if you may be eligible for school or state aid, in addition to federal aid.

How do I find out what my Expected Family Contribution (EFC) is?

Your EFC will be listed on your *Student Aid Report* (SAR). Your SAR summarizes the information you submitted on your FAFSA form. It is important to review your SAR to make sure all of your information is correct and complete. Make corrections or provide additional information, as necessary.

How much student financial aid will I receive?

Using the information on your FAFSA form and your EFC, the financial aid office at your college will determine the amount of aid you will receive. The college will use your EFC to prepare a financial aid package to help you meet your financial need. Financial need is the difference between the cost of attendance (which can include living expenses), as determined by your college, and your EFC. If you are eligible for a Federal Pell Grant, you may receive it from only one college for the same period of enrollment. If you or your family have unusual circumstances that should be taken into account, contact your college's financial aid office. Some examples of unusual circumstances are: unusual medical or dental expenses or a large change in income from 2020 to this year.

When will I receive the student financial aid?

Any financial aid you are eligible to receive will be paid to you through your college. Typically, your college will first use the aid to pay tuition, fees and room and board (if provided by the college). Any remaining aid is paid to you for your other educational expenses.

How can I have more colleges receive my FAFSA form information?

If you are completing a paper FAFSA form, you can only list four colleges in the school code step. You may add more colleges by doing one of the following:

- After your FAFSA form has been processed, go to **fafsa.gov**, log in to the site, and follow the instructions for correcting your FAFSA form.

- Use the SAR which you will receive after your FAFSA form is processed. Your Data Release Number (DRN) verifies your identity and will be listed on the first page of your SAR. You can call 1-800-433-3243 and provide your DRN to a customer service representative, who will add more school codes for you.

- Provide your DRN to the financial aid administrator at the college you want added, and he or she can add their school code to your FAFSA form.

Note: Your FAFSA record can only list up to ten school codes. If there are ten school codes on your record, each new code will need to replace one of the school codes listed.

Where can I receive more information on student financial aid?

The best place for information about student financial aid is the financial aid office at the college you plan to attend. The financial aid administrator can tell you about student aid available from your state, the college itself and other sources.

- You can also visit our web site **StudentAid.gov**.
- For information by phone you can call our Federal Student Aid Information Center at 1-800-433-3243.
- You can also check with your high school counselor, your state aid agency or your local library's reference section.

Information about other nonfederal assistance may be available from foundations, faith-based organizations, community organizations and civic groups, as well as organizations related to your field of interest, such as the American Medical Association or American Bar Association. Check with your parents' employers or unions to see if they award scholarships or have tuition assistance plans.

FAFSA® Privacy Act Statement

Authority: Sections 483 and 484 of the Higher Education Act of 1965, as amended, give us the authority to ask these questions, and to collect Social Security numbers (SSN), from both you and your parents.

Purpose: We use the information provided on your *Free Application for Federal Student Aid* (FAFSA®) form to determine if you are eligible to receive federal student aid and the amount that you are eligible to receive. Your SSN is used to verify your identity and retrieve your records. We may request your SSN again for these purposes. State and institutional student financial aid programs also may use the information provided on your FAFSA form to determine if you are eligible to receive state and institutional aid and the financial need that you have for such aid.

Routine Uses: The information you provide will not be disclosed outside of the U.S. Department of Education (Department), except with your consent, and as otherwise allowed by the Privacy Act of 1974, 5 U.S.C. 552a, as amended, pursuant to the routine uses identified in the Federal Student Aid Application File System of Records Notice **federalregister.gov/documents/2020/10/29/2020-23581/privacy-act-of-1974-system-of-records**. A routine use is a disclosure to a third party without your consent. The Department may disclose your information to third parties under a routine use published in the Notice linked to above. Significant routine use disclosures are as follows:

- Under the published routine uses, we may disclose information to third parties that we have authorized to assist the Department in administering the federal student financial aid programs.

- The Department also may send your information to other federal agencies through computer matching programs to verify your eligibility for federal student financial aid, to perform debt collection under the federal loan programs, and to minimize and prevent waste, fraud, and abuse in the federal student aid programs. Such computer matching programs include matching programs with the Selective Service System, Social Security Administration, Department of Veterans Affairs, Department of Homeland Security, Department of Justice, the Department of Defense, and the Department of Housing and Urban Development. More information on sharing with other federal agencies pursuant to a computer matching agreement can be found on the Department of Education's Computer Matching Agreements page **www2.ed.gov/about/offices/list/om/pirms/cma.html**.

- The Department will send your information to the state higher education agency in your state of legal residence. This disclosure will allow you to apply for state student financial aid without necessarily having to submit an additional application form. Your application information also will be sent to the college(s) listed on your FAFSA form, or its representative, and to the state higher education agencies in the states of the colleges listed. Additional information on state higher education agencies can be found at **www2.ed.gov/about/contacts/state/index.html**

- The Department may also disclose information to your parents or spouse and to members of Congress if you ask them to help you with student aid questions. If the federal government, the U.S. Department of Education, or an employee of the U.S. Department of Education is involved in litigation, we may send information to the Department of Justice, or a court or adjudicative body, if the disclosure is related to financial aid and certain conditions are met. In addition, we may send your information to a foreign, federal, state, or local enforcement agency if the information that you submitted indicates a violation or potential violation of law, for which that agency has jurisdiction for investigation or prosecution. We may send information to the Office of Management and Budget or the Congressional Budget Service to fulfill Fair Credit Reporting Act requirements. Finally, we may disclose records in the course of responding to a breach of data to appropriate agencies, entities, and persons.

- The Department may disclose information to a federal or state agency or a fiscal or financial agency designated by the U.S. Department of the Treasury for the purposes of identifying, preventing, or recouping an improper payment.

- We may send information regarding a claim that is determined to be valid and overdue to a consumer reporting agency. This information includes identifiers from the record; the amount, status and history of the claim; and the program under which the claim arose.

Effects of Not Providing Information: Providing information, including your SSN, is voluntary; however, if you do not give us all the information we need to process your FAFSA form, your aid may be delayed or denied. If you are applying solely for federal aid, you must answer all of the following questions that apply to you and are requested: 1–9, 14–16, 18, 21–23, 26, 28–29, 32–58, 60–67, 72–100, 102, and 103. If you want to apply for state financial aid, you must answer all the relevant questions.

State Certification: By submitting this application, you are giving your state financial aid agency permission to verify any statement on this form and to obtain income tax information for all persons required to report income on this form.

The Paperwork Reduction Act of 1995: According to the Paperwork Reduction Act of 1995, no persons are required to respond to a collection of information unless such collection displays a valid OMB control number. The valid OMB control number for this information collection is 1845-0001. Public reporting burden for this collection of information is estimated to average one and a half hours per response, including time for reviewing instructions, searching existing data sources, gathering and maintaining the data needed, and completing and reviewing the collection of information. The obligation to respond to this collection is voluntary. If you have comments or concerns regarding the status of your individual submission of this form, please contact the Federal Student Aid Information Center, P.O. Box 84, Washington, D.C. 20044 directly. (Note: Please do not return the completed form to this address.)

We may request additional information from you to process your application more efficiently. We will collect this additional information only as needed and on a voluntary basis.

FAFSA®

July 1, 2022 – June 30, 2023

FREE APPLICATION *for* FEDERAL STUDENT AID

Federal Student Aid
An OFFICE of the U.S. DEPARTMENT of EDUCATION

PROUD SPONSOR of
the AMERICAN MIND®

Step One (Student): For questions 1-31, leave any questions that do not apply to you (the student) blank.

OMB # 1845-0001

Your full name (**exactly as it appears on your Social Security card**) If your name has a suffix, such as Jr. or III, include a space between your last name and suffix.

1. Last name

2. First name

3. Middle initial

Your permanent mailing address

4. Number and street (include apt. number)

5. City (and country if not U.S.)

6. State

7. ZIP code

8. Your Social Security Number **See Notes page 9.**

9. Your date of birth MONTH DAY YEAR

10. Your telephone number ( )

Your driver's license number and driver's license state (if you have one)

11. Driver's license number

12. Driver's license state

13. Your e-mail address. If you provide your e-mail address, we will communicate with you electronically. For example, when your FAFSA form has been processed, you will be notified by e-mail. Your e-mail address will also be shared with your state and the colleges listed on your FAFSA form to allow them to communicate with you. If you do not have an e-mail address, leave this field blank.

14. Are you a U.S. citizen? Mark only one. **See Notes page 9.**
- Yes, I am a U.S. citizen (U.S. national). **Skip to question 16.** ...... ○ 1
- No, but I am an eligible noncitizen. **Fill in question 15.** .... ○ 2
- No, I am not a citizen or eligible noncitizen. **Skip to question 16.** ○ 3

15. Alien Registration Number
A

16. What is your marital status as of today? **See Notes page 9.**
- I am single .... ○ 1
- I am married/remarried ○ 2
- I am separated .... ○ 3
- I am divorced or widowed ○ 4

17. Month and year you were married, remarried, separated, divorced or widowed. **See Notes page 9.** MONTH YEAR

18. What is your state of legal residence? STATE

19. Did you become a legal resident of this state before January 1, 2017?
- Yes ○ 1
- No ○ 2

20. If the answer to question 19 is "No," give month and year you became a legal resident of that state. MONTH YEAR

21. Are you male or female? **See Notes page 9.**
- Male ○ 1
- Female ○ 2

22. **If female, skip to question 23.** Most male students must register with the Selective Service System. If you are male, are age 18-25, and have not registered, fill in the circle and we will register you. **See Notes page 9.**
- Register me ○ 1

23. Have you been convicted for the possession or sale of illegal drugs for an offense that occurred while you were receiving federal student aid (such as grants, work-study, or loans)?
Answer "No" if you have never received federal student aid or if you have never had a drug conviction for an offense that occurred while receiving federal student aid. If you have a drug conviction for an offense that occurred while you were receiving federal student aid, answer "Yes." A recently passed law means that you are now eligible for federal student aid even if you have been convicted for the sale or possession of illegal drugs while receiving federal student aid. No further action is required.
- No ○ 1
- Yes ○ 3

Some states and colleges offer aid based on the level of schooling your parents completed.

24. Highest school completed by Parent 1
- Middle school/Jr. high ○ 1
- High school ○ 2
- College or beyond ○ 3
- Other/unknown ○ 4

25. Highest school completed by Parent 2
- Middle school/Jr. high ○ 1
- High school ○ 2
- College or beyond ○ 3
- Other/unknown ○ 4

26. What will your high school completion status be when you begin college in the 2022-2023 school year?
- High school diploma. **Answer question 27** .... ○ 1
- General Educational Development (GED) certificate or state certificate. **Skip to question 28.** ○ 2
- Homeschooled. **Skip to question 28.** .... ○ 3
- None of the above. **Skip to question 28.** .... ○ 4

27. What is the name of the high school where you received or will receive your high school diploma? Enter the complete high school name, and the city and state where the high school is located.

High School Name

High School City

STATE

28. Will you have your first bachelor's degree before you begin the 2022-2023 school year?

Yes ◯ 1   No ◯ 2

29. What will your college grade level be when you begin the 2022-2023 school year?

Never attended college and 1st year undergraduate .... ◯ 0

Attended college before and 1st year undergraduate .... ◯ 1

2nd year undergraduate/sophomore .... ◯ 2

3rd year undergraduate/junior .... ◯ 3

4th year undergraduate/senior .... ◯ 4

5th year/other undergraduate .... ◯ 5

1st year college graduate/professional (MBA, MD, PhD, etc.) .... ◯ 6

Continuing graduate/professional or beyond (MBA, MD, PhD, etc.) .. ◯ 7

30. What college degree or certificate will you be working on when you begin the 2022-2023 school year?

1st bachelor's degree .... ◯ 1

2nd bachelor's degree .... ◯ 2

Associate degree (occupational or technical program) .... ◯ 3

Associate degree (general education or transfer program)................. ◯ 4

Certificate or diploma (occupational, technical or education program of less than two years)... ◯ 5

Certificate or diploma (occupational, technical or education program of two or more years) .... ◯ 6

Teaching credential (nondegree program)................................ ◯ 7

College graduate or professional degree (MBA, MD, PhD, etc.) .... ◯ 8

Other/undecided .... ◯ 9

31. Are you interested in being considered for work-study?   Yes ◯ 1 No ◯ 2 Don't know ◯ 3

Step Two (Student): Answer questions 32–57 about yourself (the student). If you were never married, or are separated, divorced or widowed and are not remarried, answer only about yourself. If you are married or remarried as of today, include information about your spouse.

32. For 2020, have you (the student) completed your IRS income tax return or another tax return listed in question 33?

I have already completed my return .... ◯ 1

I will file but have not yet completed my return .... ◯ 2

I'm not going to file. **Skip to question 38.** ◯ 3

33. What income tax return did you file or will you file for 2020?

IRS 1040 .... ◯ 1

A foreign tax return or IRS 1040NR. **See Notes page 9.** .... ◯ 3

A tax return with Puerto Rico, another U.S. territory, or Freely Associated State. **See Notes page 9.** ...... ◯ 4

34. For 2020, what is or will be your tax filing status according to your tax return?

Single .... ◯ 1

Head of household................... ◯ 4

Married—filed joint return .... ◯ 2

Married—filed separate return .... ◯ 3

Qualifying widow(er)................. ◯ 5

Don't know .... ◯ 6

35. Did (or will) you file a Schedule 1 with your 2020 tax return? Answer "**No**" if you did not file a Schedule 1 or **only filed** a Schedule 1 to report: unemployment compensation, educator expenses, IRA deduction, student loan interest deduction, or Alaska Permanent Fund dividend. **See Notes page 9.**   Yes ◯ 2 No ◯ 1 Don't know ◯ 3

For questions 36–44, if the answer is zero or the question does not apply to you, enter 0. Report whole dollar amounts with no cents.

36. What was your (and spouse's) adjusted gross income for 2020? Adjusted gross income is on IRS Form 1040—line 11. $ ⬚⬚⬚⬚⬚⬚⬚

37. Enter your (and spouse's) income tax for 2020. Income tax amount is the total of IRS Form 1040—line 22 minus Schedule 2—line 2. If negative, enter a zero here. $ ⬚⬚⬚⬚⬚⬚⬚

Questions 38 and 39 ask about earnings (wages, salaries, tips, etc.) in 2020. Answer the questions whether or not a tax return was filed. This information may be on the W-2 forms or on the tax return selected in question 33: IRS Form 1040—line 1 + Schedule 1—lines 3 + 6 + Schedule K-1 (IRS Form 1065)—Box 14 (Code A). If any individual earning item is negative, do not include that item in your calculation.

38. How much did you earn from working in 2020? $ ⬚⬚⬚⬚⬚⬚⬚

39. How much did your spouse earn from working in 2020? $ ⬚⬚⬚⬚⬚⬚⬚

40. As of today, what is your (and spouse's) total current balance of cash, savings, and checking accounts? **Don't include** student financial aid. $ ⬚⬚⬚⬚⬚⬚⬚

41. As of today, what is the net worth of your (and spouse's) investments, including real estate? **Don't include** the home you live in. **See Notes page 9.** $ ⬚⬚⬚⬚⬚⬚⬚

42. As of today, what is the net worth of your (and spouse's) current businesses and/or investment farms? **Don't include** a family farm or family business with 100 or fewer full-time or full-time equivalent employees. **See Notes page 9.** $ ⬚⬚⬚⬚⬚⬚⬚

43. Student's 2020 Additional Financial Information (Enter the combined amounts for you and your spouse.)

   a. Education credits (American Opportunity Tax Credit and Lifetime Learning Tax Credit) from IRS Form 1040 Schedule 3—line 3. $

   b. Child support paid because of divorce or separation or as a result of a legal requirement. **Don't include** support for children in your household, as reported in question 93. $

   c. Taxable earnings from need-based employment programs, such as Federal Work-Study and need-based employment portions of fellowships and assistantships. $

   d. Taxable college grant and scholarship aid **reported to the IRS as income**. Includes AmeriCorps benefits (awards, living allowances and interest accrual payments), as well as grant and scholarship portions of fellowships and assistantships. $

   e. Combat pay or special combat pay. Only enter the amount that was taxable and included in your adjusted gross income. **Don't include** untaxed combat pay. $

   f. Earnings from work under a cooperative education program offered by a college. $

44. Student's 2020 Untaxed Income (Enter the combined amounts for you and your spouse.)

   a. Payments to tax-deferred pension and retirement savings plans (paid directly or withheld from earnings), including, but not limited to, amounts reported on the W-2 forms in Boxes 12a through 12d, codes D, E, F, G, H and S. **Don't include** amounts reported in code DD (employer contributions toward employee health benefits). $

   b. IRA deductions and payments to self-employed SEP, SIMPLE, Keogh and other qualified plans from IRS Form 1040 Schedule 1—total of lines 15 + 19. $

   c. Child support received for any of your children. **Don't include** foster care or adoption payments. $

   d. Tax exempt interest income from IRS Form 1040—line 2a. $

   e. Untaxed portions of IRA distributions and pensions from IRS Form 1040—(lines 4a + 5a) minus (lines 4b + 5b). **Exclude rollovers.** If negative, enter a zero here. $

   f. Housing, food and other living allowances paid to members of the military, clergy and others (including cash payments and cash value of benefits). **Don't include** the value of on-base military housing or the value of a basic military allowance for housing. $

   g. Veterans noneducation benefits, such as Disability, Death Pension, or Dependency & Indemnity Compensation (DIC) and/or VA Educational Work-Study allowances. $

   h. Other untaxed income not reported in items 44a through 44g, such as workers' compensation, disability benefits, untaxed foreign income, etc. Also include the untaxed portions of health savings accounts from IRS Form 1040 Schedule 1—line 12. **Don't include** extended foster care benefits, student aid, earned income credit, additional child tax credit, welfare payments, untaxed Social Security benefits, Supplemental Security Income, Workforce Innovation and Opportunity Act educational benefits, on-base military housing or a military housing allowance, combat pay, benefits from flexible spending arrangements (e.g., cafeteria plans), foreign income exclusion or credit for federal tax on special fuels. $

   i. Money received, or paid on your behalf (e.g., bills), not reported elsewhere on this form. This includes money that you received from a parent or other person whose financial information is not reported on this form and that is not part of a legal child support agreement. **See Notes page 9**. $

Step Three (Student):
Answer the questions in this step to determine if you will need to provide parental information. Once you answer **"Yes" to any** of the questions in this step, skip Step Four and go to Step Five on page 8.

45. Were you born before January 1, 1999? .... Yes ○ 1 No ○ 2

46. As of today, are you married? (Also answer "Yes" if you are separated but not divorced.) .... Yes ○ 1 No ○ 2

47. At the beginning of the 2022-2023 school year, will you be working on a master's or doctorate program (such as an MA, MBA, MD, JD, PhD, EdD, graduate certificate, etc.)?.. Yes ○ 1 No ○ 2

48. Are you currently serving on active duty in the U.S. Armed Forces for purposes other than training? **See Notes page 9**. .... Yes ○ 1 No ○ 2

49. Are you a veteran of the U.S. Armed Forces? **See Notes page 9**.. Yes ○ 1 No ○ 2

50. Do you now have or will you have children who will receive more than half of their support from you between July 1, 2022 and June 30, 2023?... Yes ○ 1 No ○ 2

51. Do you have dependents (other than your children or spouse) who live with you and who receive more than half of their support from you, now and through June 30, 2023? .... Yes ○ 1 No ○ 2

52. At any time since you turned age 13, were both your parents deceased, were you in foster care or were you a dependent or ward of the court? **See Notes page 10**... Yes ○ 1 No ○ 2

53. As determined by a court in your state of legal residence, are you or were you an emancipated minor? **See Notes page 10**. .. Yes ○ 1 No ○ 2

54. Does someone other than your parent or stepparent have legal guardianship of you, as determined by a court in your state of legal residence? **See Notes page 10**. .... Yes ○ 1 No ○ 2

55. At any time on or after July 1, 2021, did your high school or school district homeless liaison determine that you were an unaccompanied youth who was homeless or were self-supporting and at risk of being homeless? **See Notes page 10**...... Yes ○ 1 No ○ 2

56. At any time on or after July 1, 2021, did the director of an emergency shelter or transitional housing program funded by the U.S. Department of Housing and Urban Development determine that you were an unaccompanied youth who was homeless or were self-supporting and at risk of being homeless? **See Notes page 10**. .... Yes ○ 1 No ○ 2

57. At any time on or after July 1, 2021, did the director of a runaway or homeless youth basic center or transitional living program determine that you were an unaccompanied youth who were homeless or were self-supporting and at risk of being homeless? **See Notes page 10**. .... Yes ○ 1 No ○ 2

If you (the student) answered "No" to every question in Step Three, go to Step Four.
If you answered "Yes" to any question in Step Three, skip Step Four and go to Step Five on page 8.
(Health professions and law school students: Your college may require you to complete Step Four even if you answered "Yes" to any Step Three question.)
If you believe that you are unable to provide parental information, see Notes page 10.

Step Four (Parent): Complete this step if you (the student) answered "No" to all questions in Step Three.

Answer all the questions in Step Four even if you do not live with your legal parents (biological, adoptive, or as determined by the state [for example, if the parent is listed on the birth certificate]). Grandparents, foster parents, legal guardians, widowed stepparents, aunts, uncles, and siblings are not considered parents on this form unless they have legally adopted you. If your legal parents are married to each other, or are not married to each other and **live together**, answer the questions about both of them. If your parent was never married or is remarried, divorced, separated or widowed, **see StudentAid.gov/fafsa-parent** and/or **Notes page 10** for additional instructions.

58. As of today, what is the marital status of your parents?

Never married..................... ○ 2   Married or remarried............... ○ 1

Unmarried and both legal parents living together........................... ○ 5   Divorced or separated.............. ○ 3

Widowed.......................... ○ 4

59. Month and year they were married, remarried, separated, divorced or widowed.

MONTH | YEAR

What are the Social Security Numbers, names and dates of birth of the parents reporting information on this form? If your parent does not have a Social Security Number, you must enter 000-00-0000. Don't enter an Individual Taxpayer Identification Number (ITIN) in the Social Security Number field. If the name includes a suffix, such as Jr. or III, include a space between the last name and suffix. Enter two digits for each day and month (e.g., for May 31, enter 05 31).

Questions 60-63 are for Parent 1 (father/mother/stepparent)
60. SOCIAL SECURITY NUMBER   **61.** LAST NAME, AND   **62.** FIRST INITIAL   **63.** DATE OF BIRTH

Questions 64-67 are for Parent 2 (father/mother/stepparent)
64. SOCIAL SECURITY NUMBER   **65.** LAST NAME, AND   **66.** FIRST INITIAL   **67.** DATE OF BIRTH

68. Your parents' e-mail address. If you provide your parents' e-mail address, we will let them know your FAFSA form has been processed. This e-mail address will also be shared with your state and the colleges listed on your FAFSA form to allow them to electronically communicate with your parents.

69. What is your parents' state of legal residence?   STATE

70. Did your parents become legal residents of this state before January 1, 2017?   Yes ○ 1   No ○ 2

71. If the answer to question 70 is "No," give the month and year legal residency began for the parent who has lived in the state the longest.   MONTH | YEAR

72. How many people are in your parents' household?
Include:
- yourself, even if you don't live with your parents,
- your parents,
- your parents' other children (even if they do not live with your parents) if (a) your parents will provide more than half of their support between July 1, 2022 and June 30, 2023, or (b) the children could answer "No" to every question in Step Three on page 5 of this form, and
- other people if they now live with your parents, your parents provide more than half of their support and your parents will continue to provide more than half of their support between July 1, 2022 and June 30, 2023.

73. How many people in your parents' household (from question 72) will be college students between July 1, 2022 and June 30, 2023? Always count yourself as a college student. Do not include your parents. Do not include siblings who are in U.S. military service academies. You may include others only if they will attend, at least half-time in 2022-2023, a program that leads to a college degree or certificate.

At any time during 2020 or 2021, did you, your parents, or anyone in your parents' household (from question 72) receive benefits from any of the federal programs listed? Mark all that apply. Answering these questions will NOT reduce eligibility for student aid or these programs. TANF has different names in many states. Call 1-800-433-3243 to find out the name of your state's program. If you, your parents, or anyone in your household receives any of these benefits after filing the FAFSA form but before December 31, 2021, you must update your response by logging in to **fafsa.gov** and selecting "Make FAFSA Corrections."

74. Medicaid or Supplemental Security Income (SSI) ○

75. Supplemental Nutrition Assistance Program (SNAP) ○

76. Free or Reduced Price School Lunch ○

77. Temporary Assistance for Needy Families (TANF) ○

78. Special Supplemental Nutrition Program for Women, Infants, and Children (WIC) ○

If your answer to question 58 was "Unmarried and both legal parents living together," contact 1-800-433-3243 for help with questions 79-92.

79. For 2020, have your parents completed their IRS income tax return or another tax return listed in question 80?

My parents have already completed their return. ○ 1

My parents will file but have not yet completed their return.................... ○ 2

My parents are not going to file. **Skip to question 86**................ ○ 3

80. What income tax return did your parents file or will they file for 2020?

IRS 1040................................. ○ 1

A foreign tax return or IRS 1040NR. **See Notes page 9**..................... ○ 3

A tax return with Puerto Rico, another U.S. territory or Freely Associated State. **See Notes page 9**. .... ○ 4

81. For 2020, what is or will be your parents' tax filing status according to their tax return?

Single .... ○ 1
Head of household.................. ○ 4
Married—filed joint return .... ○ 2
Married—filed separate return ...... ○ 3
Qualifying widow(er).............. ○ 5
Don't know .... ○ 6

82. Did (or will) your parents file a Schedule 1 with their 2020 tax return? Answer **"No"** if they did not file a Schedule 1 or **only filed** a Schedule 1 to report: unemployment compensation, educator expenses, IRA deduction, student loan interest deduction, or Alaska Permanent Fund dividend. **See Notes page 9.**   Yes ○ 2   No ○ 1   Don't know ○ 3

83. As of today, is either of your parents a dislocated worker? **See Notes page 10.**   Yes ○ 1   No ○ 2   Don't know ○ 3

For questions 84–92, if the answer is zero or the question does not apply, enter 0. Report whole dollar amounts with no cents.

84. What was your parents' adjusted gross income for 2020? Adjusted gross income is on IRS Form 1040—line 11. $ ☐☐☐,☐☐☐

85. Enter your parents' income tax for 2020. Income tax amount is the total of IRS Form 1040—line 22 minus Schedule 2—line 2. If negative, enter a zero here. $ ☐☐☐,☐☐☐

Questions 86 and 87 ask about earnings (wages, salaries, tips, etc.) in 2020. Answer the questions whether or not a tax return was filed. This information may be on the W-2 forms or on the tax return selected in question 80: IRS Form 1040—line 1 + Schedule 1—lines 3 + 6 + Schedule K-1 (IRS Form 1065)—Box 14 (Code A). If any individual earning item is negative, do not include that item in your calculation. Report the information for the parent listed in questions 60-63 in question 86 and the information for the parent listed in questions 64-67 in question 87.

86. How much did Parent 1 (father/mother/stepparent) earn from working in 2020? $ ☐☐☐,☐☐☐

87. How much did Parent 2 (father/mother/stepparent) earn from working in 2020? $ ☐☐☐,☐☐☐

88. As of today, what is your parents' total current balance of cash, savings, and checking accounts? **Don't include** student financial aid. $ ☐☐☐,☐☐☐

89. As of today, what is the net worth of your parents' investments, including real estate? **Don't include** the home in which your parents live. **See Notes page 9.** $ ☐☐☐,☐☐☐

90. As of today, what is the net worth of your parents' current businesses and/or investment farms? **Don't include** a family farm or family business with 100 or fewer full-time or full-time equivalent employees. **See Notes page 9.** $ ☐☐☐,☐☐☐

91. Parents' 2020 Additional Financial Information (Enter the amounts for your parent[s].)

a. Education credits (American Opportunity Tax Credit and Lifetime Learning Tax Credit) from IRS Form 1040 Schedule 3—line 3. $ ☐☐☐,☐☐☐

b. Child support paid because of divorce or separation or as a result of a legal requirement. **Don't include** support for children in your parents' household, as reported in question 72. $ ☐☐☐,☐☐☐

c. Your parents' taxable earnings from need-based employment programs, such as Federal Work-Study and need-based employment portions of fellowships and assistantships. $ ☐☐☐,☐☐☐

d. Your parents' taxable college grant and scholarship aid **reported to the IRS as income**. Includes AmeriCorps benefits (awards, living allowances and interest accrual payments), as well as grant and scholarship portions of fellowships and assistantships. $ ☐☐☐,☐☐☐

e. Combat pay or special combat pay. Only enter the amount that was taxable and included in your parents' adjusted gross income. **Don't include** untaxed combat pay. $ ☐☐☐,☐☐☐

f. Earnings from work under a cooperative education program offered by a college. $ ☐☐☐,☐☐☐

92. Parents' 2020 Untaxed Income (Enter the amounts for your parent[s].)

a. Payments to tax-deferred pension and retirement savings plans (paid directly or withheld from earnings), including, but not limited to, amounts reported on the W-2 forms in Boxes 12a through 12d, codes D, E, F, G, H and S. **Don't include** amounts reported in code DD (employer contributions toward employee health benefits). $ ☐☐☐,☐☐☐

b. IRA deductions and payments to self-employed SEP, SIMPLE, Keogh and other qualified plans from IRS Form 1040 Schedule 1—total of lines 15 + 19. $ ☐☐☐,☐☐☐

c. Child support received for any of your parents' children. **Don't include** foster care or adoption payments. $ ☐☐☐,☐☐☐

d. Tax exempt interest income from IRS Form 1040—line 2a. $ ☐☐☐,☐☐☐

e. Untaxed portions of IRA distributions and pensions from IRS Form 1040—(lines 4a + 5a) minus (lines 4b + 5b). **Exclude rollovers.** If negative, enter a zero here. $ ☐☐☐,☐☐☐

f. Housing, food and other living allowances paid to members of the military, clergy and others (including cash payments and cash value of benefits). **Don't include** the value of on-base military housing or the value of a basic military allowance for housing. $ ☐☐☐,☐☐☐

g. Veterans noneducation benefits, such as Disability, Death Pension, or Dependency & Indemnity Compensation (DIC) and/or VA Educational Work-Study allowances. $ ☐☐☐,☐☐☐

h. Other untaxed income not reported in items 92a through 92g, such as workers' compensation, disability benefits, untaxed foreign income, etc. Also include the untaxed portions of health savings accounts from IRS Form 1040 Schedule 1—line 12. **Don't include** extended foster care benefits, student aid, earned income credit, additional child tax credit, welfare payments, untaxed Social Security benefits, Supplemental Security Income, Workforce Innovation and Opportunity Act educational benefits, on-base military housing or a military housing allowance, combat pay, benefits from flexible spending arrangements (e.g., cafeteria plans), foreign income exclusion or credit for federal tax on special fuels. $ ☐☐☐,☐☐☐

Step Five (Student): Complete this step only if you (the student) answered "Yes" to any questions in Step Three.

93. How many people are in your household?
Include:
- yourself (and your spouse),
- your children, if you will provide more than half of their support between July 1, 2022 and June 30, 2023, even if they do not live with you, and
- other people if they now live with you, you provide more than half of their support and you will continue to provide more than half of their support between July 1, 2022 and June 30, 2023.

94. How many people in your (and your spouse's) household (from question 93) will be college students between July 1, 2022 and June 30, 2023? Always count yourself as a college student. Do not include family members who are in U.S. military service academies. Include others only if they will attend, at least half-time in 2022-2023, a program that leads to a college degree or certificate.

At any time during 2020 or 2021, did you (or your spouse) or anyone in your household (from question 93) receive benefits from any of the federal programs listed?
Mark all that apply. Answering these questions will NOT reduce eligibility for student aid or these programs. TANF has different names in many states. Call 1-800-433-3243 to find out the name of your state's program. If you (or your spouse) or anyone in your household receives any of these benefits after filing the FAFSA form but before December 31, 2021, you must update your response by logging in to **fafsa.gov** and selecting "Make FAFSA Corrections."

95. Medicaid or Supplemental Security Income (SSI) ○

96. Supplemental Nutrition Assistance Program (SNAP) ○

97. Free or Reduced Price School Lunch ○

98. Temporary Assistance for Needy Families (TANF) ○

99. Special Supplemental Nutrition Program for Women, Infants, and Children (WIC) ○

100. As of today, are you (or your spouse) a dislocated worker? **See Notes page 10.**   Yes ○ 1   No ○ 2   Don't know ○ 3

Step Six (Student): Indicate which colleges you want to receive your FAFSA information.

Enter the six-digit federal school code and your housing plans for each college or school you want to receive your FAFSA information. You can find the school codes at **fafsa.gov/schoolsearch** or by calling 1-800-433-3243. If you cannot obtain a code, write in the complete name, address, city and state of the college. If you want more schools to receive your FAFSA information, read *What is the FAFSA form?* on page 2. All of the information you included on your FAFSA form, *with the exception of the list of colleges*, will be sent to each of the colleges you listed. In addition, all of your FAFSA information, *including the list of colleges*, will be sent to your state grant agency. For federal student aid purposes, it does not matter in what order you list your selected schools. However, the order in which you list schools may affect your eligibility for state aid. Consult your state agency or **StudentAid.gov/order** for details.

101.a 1ST FEDERAL SCHOOL CODE | OR | NAME OF COLLEGE / ADDRESS AND CITY | STATE | HOUSING PLANS
101.b on campus ○ 1 / with parent ○ 2 / off campus ○ 3

101.c 2ND FEDERAL SCHOOL CODE | OR | NAME OF COLLEGE / ADDRESS AND CITY | STATE
101.d on campus ○ 1 / with parent ○ 2 / off campus ○ 3

101.e 3RD FEDERAL SCHOOL CODE | OR | NAME OF COLLEGE / ADDRESS AND CITY | STATE
101.f on campus ○ 1 / with parent ○ 2 / off campus ○ 3

101.g 4TH FEDERAL SCHOOL CODE | OR | NAME OF COLLEGE / ADDRESS AND CITY | STATE
101.h on campus ○ 1 / with parent ○ 2 / off campus ○ 3

Step Seven (Student and Parent): Read, sign and date.

If you are the student, by signing this application you certify that you (1) will use federal and/or state student financial aid only to pay the cost of attending an institution of higher education, (2) are not in default on a federal student loan or have made satisfactory arrangements to repay it, (3) do not owe money back on a federal student grant or have made satisfactory arrangements to repay it, (4) will notify your college if you default on a federal student loan and (5) will not receive a Federal Pell Grant from more than one college for the same period of time.

If you are the parent or the student, by signing this application you certify that all of the information you provided is true and complete to the best of your knowledge and you agree, if asked, to provide information that will verify the accuracy of your completed form. This information may include U.S. or state income tax forms that you filed or are required to file. Also, you certify that you understand that **the Secretary of Education has the authority to verify information reported on this application with the Internal Revenue Service and other federal agencies.** If you electronically sign any document related to the federal student aid programs using an FSA ID (username and password) and/or any other credential, you certify that you are the person identified by that username and password and/or other credential, and have not disclosed that username and password and/or other credential to anyone else. If you purposely give false or misleading information, you may be fined up to $20,000, sent to prison, or both.

102. Date this form was completed
MONTH   DAY   2021 ○   2022 ○   2023 ○

103. Student (Sign below)
1

Parent (A parent from Step Four sign below.)
2

If a fee was paid to someone for advice or for completing this form, that person must complete this section.

Preparer's name, firm and address

104. Preparer's Social Security Number (or 105)
— —

105. Employer ID number (or 104)
—

106. Preparer's signature and date
1

COLLEGE USE ONLY   FEDERAL SCHOOL CODE
D/O ○ 1   Homeless Youth Determination ○ 4

FAA Signature
1

DATA ENTRY USE ONLY: ○ P   ○ *   ○ L   ○ E

Notes for question 8 (page 3)

Enter your Social Security Number (SSN) as it appears on your Social Security card. If you are a resident of one of the Freely Associated States (i.e., the Republic of Palau, the Republic of the Marshall Islands, or the Federated States of Micronesia) and were issued an identification number beginning with "666" when submitting a FAFSA form previously, enter that number here. If you are a first-time applicant from one of the Freely Associated States, enter "666" in the first three boxes of the Social Security Number field and leave the remaining six positions blank, and we will create an identification number to be used for federal student aid purposes. Do not enter an Individual Taxpayer Identification Number (ITIN) in the Social Security Number field.

Notes for questions 14 and 15 (page 3)

If you are an eligible noncitizen, write in your eight- or nine-digit Alien Registration Number. Generally, you are an eligible noncitizen if you are (1) a permanent U.S. resident with a Permanent Resident Card (I-551); (2) a conditional permanent resident with a Conditional Green Card (I-551C); (3) the holder of an Arrival-Departure Record (I-94) from the Department of Homeland Security showing any one of the following designations: "Refugee," "Asylum Granted," "Parolee" (I-94 confirms that you were paroled for a minimum of one year and status has not expired), T-Visa holder (T-1, T-2, T-3, etc.) or "Cuban-Haitian Entrant;" or (4) the holder of a valid certification or eligibility letter from the Department of Health and Human Services showing a designation of "Victim of human trafficking."

If you are in the U.S. and have been granted Deferred Action for Childhood Arrivals (DACA), an F1 or F2 student visa, a J1 or J2 exchange visitor visa, or a G series visa (pertaining to international organizations), select "No, I am not a citizen or eligible noncitizen." You will not be eligible for federal student aid. If you have a Social Security Number but are not a citizen or an eligible noncitizen, including if you have been granted DACA, you should still complete the FAFSA form because you may be eligible for state or college aid.

Notes for questions 16 and 17 (page 3)

Report your marital status as of the date you sign your FAFSA form. If your marital status changes after you sign your FAFSA form, check with the **financial aid office at the college**.

Notes for questions 21 and 22 (page 3)

Male citizens and male immigrants residing in the U.S. aged 18 through 25 are required to register with the Selective Service System, with limited exceptions. The Selective Service System and the registration requirement applies to any person assigned the sex of male at birth (see **www.sss.gov/Registration-Info/Who-Registration**). The Selective Service System and the registration requirement for males preserves America's ability to provide resources in an emergency to the U.S. Armed Forces. For more information about the Selective Service System, visit **sss.gov**. Forms are available at your local U.S. Post Office.

Notes for questions 33 (page 4) and 80 (page 6)

If you filed or will file a foreign tax return or IRS 1040NR, or a tax return with Puerto Rico, another U.S. territory (e.g., Guam, American Samoa, the U.S. Virgin Islands, Swain's Island or the Northern Marianas Islands) or one of the Freely Associated States, use the information from that return to fill out this form. If you filed a foreign return, convert all monetary units to U.S. dollars, using the published exchange rate in effect for the date nearest to today's date. To view the daily exchange rates, go to **federalreserve.gov/releases/h10/current**.

Notes for questions 35 (page 4) and 82 (page 6)

Answer "**No**" if you (and if married, your spouse) did not file a Schedule 1.

Answer "**No**" if you (and if married, your spouse) did or will file a Schedule 1 to report **only one or more** of the following items:

1. Unemployment compensation (line 7)
2. Other income to report an Alaska Permanent Fund dividend (line 8 – may not be a negative value)
3. Educator expenses (line 10)
4. IRA deduction (line 19)
5. Student loan interest deduction (line 20)

Answer "**Yes**" if you (or if married, your spouse) filed or will file a Schedule 1 and reported additional income or adjustments to income on any lines **other than or in addition to** the five exceptions listed above.

If you do not know if you filed or will file a Schedule 1, select "**Don't know**."

Notes for questions 41 and 42 (page 4), 44i (page 5), and 89 and 90 (page 7)

Net worth means the current value, as of today, of investments, businesses, and/or investment farms, minus debts related to those same investments, businesses, or investment farms. When calculating net worth, use 0 for investments or properties with a negative value.

Investments include real estate (do not include the home in which you live), rental property (includes a unit within a family home that has its own entrance, kitchen, and bath rented to someone other than a family member), trust funds, UGMA and UTMA accounts, money market funds, mutual funds, certificates of deposit, stocks, stock options, bonds, other securities, installment and land sale contracts (including mortgages held), commodities, etc.

Investments also include qualified educational benefits or education savings accounts (e.g., Coverdell savings accounts, 529 college savings plans and the refund value of 529 prepaid tuition plans). For a student who does not report parental information, the accounts owned by the student (and/or the student's spouse) are reported as student investments in question 41. For a student who must report parental information, the accounts are reported as parental investments in question 89, including all accounts owned by the student and all accounts owned by the parents for any member of the household.

Money received, or paid on your behalf, also includes distributions to you (the student beneficiary) from a 529 plan that is owned by someone other than you or your parents (such as your grandparents, aunts, uncles, and non-custodial parents). You must include these distribution amounts in question 44i.

Investments do not include the home you live in, the value of life insurance, ABLE accounts, retirement plans (401[k] plans, pension funds, annuities, non-education IRAs, Keogh plans, etc.) or cash, savings and checking accounts already reported in questions 40 and 88.

Investments also do not include UGMA and UTMA accounts for which you are the custodian, but not the owner.

Investment value means the current balance or market value of these investments as of today. Investment debt means only those debts that are related to the investments.

Business and/or investment farm value includes the market value of land, buildings, machinery, equipment, inventory, etc. Business and/or investment farm debt means only those debts for which the business or investment farm was used as collateral.

Business value does not include the value of a small business if your family owns and controls more than 50 percent of the business and the business has 100 or fewer full-time or full-time equivalent employees. For small business value, your family includes (1) persons directly related to you, such as a parent, sister or cousin, or (2) persons who are or were related to you by marriage, such as a spouse, stepparent or sister-in-law.

Investment farm value does not include the value of a family farm that you (your spouse and/or your parents) live on and operate.

Notes for question 48 (page 5)

Answer "**Yes**" if you are currently serving in the U.S. Armed Forces or are a National Guard or Reserves enlistee who is on active duty for other than state or training purposes.

Answer "**No**" if you are a National Guard or Reserves enlistee who is on active duty for state or training purposes.

Notes for question 49 (page 5)

Answer "**Yes**" (you are a veteran) if you (1) have engaged in active duty (including basic training) in the U.S. Armed Forces, or are a National Guard or Reserves enlistee who was called to active duty for other than state or training purposes, or were a cadet or midshipman at one of the service academies, **and** (2) were released under a condition other than dishonorable. Also answer "**Yes**" if you are not a veteran now but will be one by June 30, 2023.

Answer "**No**" (you are not a veteran) if you (1) have never engaged in active duty (including basic training) in the U.S. Armed Forces, (2) are currently an ROTC student or a cadet or midshipman at a service academy, (3) are a National Guard or Reserves enlistee activated only for state or training purposes, or (4) were engaged in active duty in the U.S. Armed Forces but released under dishonorable conditions.

Also answer "**No**" if you are currently serving in the U.S. Armed Forces and will continue to serve through June 30, 2023.

Notes continue on Page 10.

Notes for question 52 (page 5)

Answer "**Yes**" if at any time since you turned age 13:

- You had no living parent, even if you are now adopted; or
- You were in foster care, even if you are no longer in foster care today; or
- You were a dependent or ward of the court, even if you are no longer a dependent or ward of the court today. For federal student aid purposes, someone who is incarcerated is not considered a ward of the court.

If you are not sure if you were in foster care, check with your state child welfare agency. You can find that agency's contact information at **childwelfare.gov/nfcad**.

The financial aid administrator at your school may require you to provide proof that you were in foster care or a dependent or ward of the court.

Notes for questions 53 and 54 (page 5)

The definition of legal guardianship does not include your parents, even if they were appointed by a court to be your guardians. You are also not considered a legal guardian of yourself.

Answer "**Yes**" if you can provide a copy of a court's decision that as of today you are an emancipated minor or are in legal guardianship. Also answer "**Yes**" if you can provide a copy of a court's decision that you were an emancipated minor or were in legal guardianship immediately before you reached the age of being an adult in your state. The court must be located in your state of legal residence at the time the court's decision was issued.

Answer "**No**" if you are still a minor and the court decision is no longer in effect or the court decision was not in effect at the time you became an adult. Also answer "**No**" and contact your school if custody was awarded by the courts and the court papers say "custody" (not "guardianship").

The financial aid administrator at your college may require you to provide proof that you were an emancipated minor or in legal guardianship.

Notes for questions 55–57 (page 5)

Answer "**Yes**" if you received a determination at any time on or after July 1, 2021, that you were an unaccompanied youth who was homeless or at risk of being homeless.

- "**Homeless**" means lacking fixed, regular and adequate housing. You may be homeless if you are living in shelters, parks, motels, hotels, public spaces, camping grounds, cars, abandoned buildings, or temporarily living with other people because you have nowhere else to go. Also, if you are living in any of these situations and fleeing an abusive parent, you may be considered homeless even if your parent would otherwise provide a place to live.

- "**Unaccompanied**" means you are not living in the physical custody of your parent or guardian.

Answer "**No**" if you are not homeless or at risk of being homeless, or do not have a determination. However, even if you answer "**No**" to each of questions 55, 56, and 57, you should contact the financial aid administrator at the college you plan to attend if you are either (1) homeless and unaccompanied or (2) at risk of being homeless, unaccompanied, and providing for your own living expenses - as your college financial aid office can determine that you are "homeless" and are not required to provide parental information.

The financial aid administrator at your college may require you to provide a copy of the determination if you answered "**Yes**" to any of these questions.

Notes for students unable to provide parental information on pages 6 and 7

Under very limited circumstances (for example, your parents are incarcerated; you have left home due to an abusive family environment; or you do not know where your parents are and are unable to contact them), you may be able to submit your FAFSA form without parental information. **If you are unable to provide parental information**, skip Steps Four and Five, and go to Step Six. Once you submit your FAFSA form without parental data, **you must follow up with the financial aid office at the college you plan to attend**, in order to complete your FAFSA form.

Notes for Step Four, questions 58–92 (pages 6 and 7)

Review all instructions below to determine who is considered a parent on this form:

- If your parent was never married and does not live with your other legal parent, or if your parent is widowed and not remarried, answer the questions about that parent.

- If your legal parents (biological, adoptive, or as determined by the state [for example, if the parent is listed on the birth certificate]) are not married to each other and **live together**, select "Unmarried and both legal parents living together" and provide information about both of them regardless of their gender. Do not include any person who is not married to your parent and who is not a legal or biological parent. Contact 1-800-433-3243 for assistance in completing questions 79-92, or visit **StudentAid.gov/fafsa-parent**.

- If your legal parents are married, select "Married or remarried." If your legal parents are divorced but living together, select "Unmarried and both legal parents living together." If your legal parents are separated but living together, select "Married or remarried," not "Divorced or separated."

- If your parents are divorced or separated, answer the questions about the parent you lived with more during the past 12 months. (If you did not live with one parent more than the other, give answers about the parent who provided more financial support during the past 12 months or during the most recent year that you actually received support from a parent.) **If this parent is remarried as of today, answer the questions about that parent and your stepparent.**

- If your widowed parent is remarried as of today, answer the questions about that parent and your stepparent.

Notes for questions 83 (page 6) and 100 (page 8)

In general, a person may be considered a dislocated worker if he or she:

- is receiving unemployment benefits due to being laid off or losing a job and is unlikely to return to a previous occupation;

- has been laid off or received a lay-off notice from a job;

- was self-employed but is now unemployed due to economic conditions or natural disaster; or

- is the spouse of an active duty member of the Armed Forces and has experienced a loss of employment because of relocating due to permanent change in duty station; or

- is the spouse of an active duty member of the Armed Forces and is unemployed or underemployed, and is experiencing difficulty in obtaining or upgrading employment; or

- is a displaced homemaker. A displaced homemaker is generally a person who previously provided unpaid services to the family (e.g., a stay-at-home mom or dad), is no longer supported by the spouse, is unemployed or underemployed, and is having trouble finding or upgrading employment.

Except for the spouse of an active duty member of the Armed Forces, if a person quits work, generally he or she is not considered a dislocated worker even if, for example, the person is receiving unemployment benefits.

Answer "**Yes**" to question 83 if your parent is a dislocated worker. Answer "**Yes**" to question 100 if you or your spouse is a dislocated worker.

Answer "**No**" to question 83 if your parent is not a dislocated worker. Answer "**No**" to question 100 if neither you nor your spouse is a dislocated worker.

Answer "**Don't know**" to question 83 if you are not sure whether your parent is a dislocated worker. Answer "**Don't know**" to question 100 if you are not sure whether you or your spouse is a dislocated worker. You can contact your financial aid office for assistance in answering these questions.

The financial aid administrator at your college may require you to provide proof that your parent is a dislocated worker, if you answered "**Yes**" to question 83, or that you or your spouse is a dislocated worker, if you answered "**Yes**" to question 100.

Occupational Statistics:
Entry-Level Education, On-the-Job Training, Projected Growth Rate, 2020 Median Pay

OCCUPATION	ENTRY-LEVEL EDUCATION	ON-THE-JOB TRAINING	PROJECTED GROWTH RATE	2020 MEDIAN PAY
Accountants and auditors	Bachelor's degree	None	As fast as average	$60,000 to $79,999
Actors	Some college, no degree	Long-term on-the-job training	Much faster than average	n/a
Actuaries	Bachelor's degree	Long-term on-the-job training	Much faster than average	$80,000 or more
Acupuncturists and healthcare diagnosing or treating practitioners, all other	Master's degree	None	Slower than average	$80,000 or more
Adhesive bonding machine operators and tenders	High school diploma or equivalent	Moderate-term on-the-job training	Little or no change	$30,000 to $39,999
Administrative law judges, adjudicators, and hearing officers	Doctoral or professional degree	Short-term on-the-job training	Little or no change	$80,000 or more
Administrative services and facilities managers	Bachelor's degree	None	As fast as average	$80,000 or more
Adult basic education, adult secondary education, and English as a Second Language instructors	Bachelor's degree	None	Decline	$40,000 to $59,999
Advertising and promotions managers	Bachelor's degree	None	As fast as average	$80,000 or more
Advertising sales agents	High school diploma or equivalent	Moderate-term on-the-job training	Slower than average	$40,000 to $59,999
Aerospace engineering and operations technologists and technicians	Associate's degree	None	As fast as average	$60,000 to $79,999
Aerospace engineers	Bachelor's degree	None	As fast as average	$80,000 or more
Agents and business managers of artists, performers, and athletes	Bachelor's degree	None	Much faster than average	$60,000 to $79,999
Agricultural and food science technicians	Associate's degree	Moderate-term on-the-job training	As fast as average	$40,000 to $59,999
Agricultural engineers	Bachelor's degree	None	Slower than average	$80,000 or more
Agricultural equipment operators	No formal educational credential	Moderate-term on-the-job training	Faster than average	$30,000 to $39,999
Agricultural inspectors	Bachelor's degree	Moderate-term on-the-job training	As fast as average	$40,000 to $59,999
Agricultural sciences teachers, postsecondary	Doctoral or professional degree	None	Slower than average	$80,000 or more
Agricultural workers, all other	No formal educational credential	Short-term on-the-job training	Slower than average	$30,000 to $39,999
Air traffic controllers	Associate's degree	Long-term on-the-job training	Slower than average	$80,000 or more
Aircraft cargo handling supervisors	High school diploma or equivalent	None	Faster than average	$40,000 to $59,999

OCCUPATION	ENTRY-LEVEL EDUCATION	ON-THE-JOB TRAINING	PROJECTED GROWTH RATE	2020 MEDIAN PAY
Aircraft mechanics and service technicians	Postsecondary nondegree award	None	Faster than average	$60,000 to $79,999
Aircraft service attendants and transportation workers, all other	High school diploma or equivalent	Short-term on-the-job training	Faster than average	$30,000 to $39,999
Aircraft structure, surfaces, rigging, and systems assemblers	High school diploma or equivalent	Moderate-term on-the-job training	Decline	$40,000 to $59,999
Airfield operations specialists	High school diploma or equivalent	Long-term on-the-job training	Faster than average	$40,000 to $59,999
Airline pilots, copilots, and flight engineers	Bachelor's degree	Moderate-term on-the-job training	Faster than average	$80,000 or more
Ambulance drivers and attendants, except emergency medical technicians	High school diploma or equivalent	Moderate-term on-the-job training	Much faster than average	Less than $30,000
Amusement and recreation attendants	No formal educational credential	Short-term on-the-job training	Much faster than average	Less than $30,000
Anesthesiologists	Doctoral or professional degree	Internship/ residency	Little or no change	$80,000 or more
Animal breeders	High school diploma or equivalent	Short-term on-the-job training	Decline	$40,000 to $59,999
Animal caretakers	High school diploma or equivalent	Short-term on-the-job training	Much faster than average	Less than $30,000
Animal control workers	High school diploma or equivalent	Moderate-term on-the-job training	As fast as average	$30,000 to $39,999
Animal scientists	Bachelor's degree	None	As fast as average	$60,000 to $79,999
Animal trainers	High school diploma or equivalent	Moderate-term on-the-job training	Much faster than average	$30,000 to $39,999
Anthropologists and archeologists	Master's degree	None	As fast as average	$60,000 to $79,999
Anthropology and archeology teachers, postsecondary	Doctoral or professional degree	None	As fast as average	$80,000 or more
Arbitrators, mediators, and conciliators	Bachelor's degree	Moderate-term on-the-job training	As fast as average	$60,000 to $79,999
Architects, except landscape and naval	Bachelor's degree	Internship/ residency	Slower than average	$80,000 or more
Architectural and civil drafters	Associate's degree	None	Little or no change	$40,000 to $59,999
Architectural and engineering managers	Bachelor's degree	None	Slower than average	$80,000 or more
Architecture teachers, postsecondary	Doctoral or professional degree	None	As fast as average	$80,000 or more
Archivists	Master's degree	None	Faster than average	$40,000 to $59,999
Area, ethnic, and cultural studies teachers, postsecondary	Doctoral or professional degree	None	As fast as average	$60,000 to $79,999
Art directors	Bachelor's degree	None	Faster than average	$80,000 or more
Art, drama, and music teachers, postsecondary	Master's degree	None	As fast as average	$60,000 to $79,999
Artists and related workers, all other	No formal educational credential	Long-term on-the-job training	As fast as average	$60,000 to $79,999

OCCUPATION	ENTRY-LEVEL EDUCATION	ON-THE-JOB TRAINING	PROJECTED GROWTH RATE	2020 MEDIAN PAY
Astronomers	Doctoral or professional degree	None	Slower than average	$80,000 or more
Athletes and sports competitors	No formal educational credential	Long-term on-the-job training	Much faster than average	$40,000 to $59,999
Athletic trainers	Bachelor's degree	None	Much faster than average	$40,000 to $59,999
Atmospheric and space scientists	Bachelor's degree	None	As fast as average	$80,000 or more
Atmospheric, earth, marine, and space sciences teachers, postsecondary	Doctoral or professional degree	None	As fast as average	$80,000 or more
Audio and video technicians	Postsecondary nondegree award	Short-term on-the-job training	Much faster than average	$40,000 to $59,999
Audiologists	Doctoral or professional degree	None	Much faster than average	$80,000 or more
Audiovisual equipment installers and repairers	Postsecondary nondegree award	Short-term on-the-job training	Decline	$40,000 to $59,999
Automotive and watercraft service attendants	No formal educational credential	Short-term on-the-job training	Slower than average	Less than $30,000
Automotive body and related repairers	High school diploma or equivalent	Long-term on-the-job training	Slower than average	$40,000 to $59,999
Automotive glass installers and repairers	High school diploma or equivalent	Moderate-term on-the-job training	As fast as average	$30,000 to $39,999
Automotive service technicians and mechanics	Postsecondary nondegree award	Short-term on-the-job training	Little or no change	$40,000 to $59,999
Avionics technicians	Associate's degree	None	As fast as average	$60,000 to $79,999
Baggage porters and bellhops	High school diploma or equivalent	Short-term on-the-job training	Much faster than average	Less than $30,000
Bailiffs	High school diploma or equivalent	Moderate-term on-the-job training	Little or no change	$40,000 to $59,999
Bakers	No formal educational credential	Long-term on-the-job training	As fast as average	Less than $30,000
Barbers	Postsecondary nondegree award	None	Much faster than average	$30,000 to $39,999
Bartenders	No formal educational credential	Short-term on-the-job training	Much faster than average	Less than $30,000
Bicycle repairers	High school diploma or equivalent	Moderate-term on-the-job training	Slower than average	$30,000 to $39,999
Bill and account collectors	High school diploma or equivalent	Moderate-term on-the-job training	Decline	$30,000 to $39,999
Billing and posting clerks	High school diploma or equivalent	Moderate-term on-the-job training	Slower than average	$30,000 to $39,999
Biochemists and biophysicists	Doctoral or professional degree	None	Slower than average	$80,000 or more
Bioengineers and biomedical engineers	Bachelor's degree	None	As fast as average	$80,000 or more
Biological science teachers, postsecondary	Doctoral or professional degree	None	Faster than average	$80,000 or more

OCCUPATION	ENTRY-LEVEL EDUCATION	ON-THE-JOB TRAINING	PROJECTED GROWTH RATE	2020 MEDIAN PAY
Biological scientists, all other	Bachelor's degree	None	Slower than average	$80,000 or more
Biological technicians	Bachelor's degree	None	As fast as average	$40,000 to $59,999
Boilermakers	High school diploma or equivalent	Apprenticeship	Little or no change	$60,000 to $79,999
Bookkeeping, accounting, and auditing clerks	Some college, no degree	Moderate-term on-the-job training	Decline	$40,000 to $59,999
Brickmasons and blockmasons	High school diploma or equivalent	Apprenticeship	Decline	$40,000 to $59,999
Bridge and lock tenders	High school diploma or equivalent	Short-term on-the-job training	Slower than average	$40,000 to $59,999
Broadcast announcers and radio disc jockeys	Bachelor's degree	None	As fast as average	$30,000 to $39,999
Broadcast technicians	Associate's degree	Short-term on-the-job training	Faster than average	$40,000 to $59,999
Brokerage clerks	High school diploma or equivalent	Moderate-term on-the-job training	Decline	$40,000 to $59,999
Budget analysts	Bachelor's degree	None	Slower than average	$60,000 to $79,999
Building cleaning workers, all other	No formal educational credential	Short-term on-the-job training	Slower than average	$30,000 to $39,999
Bus and truck mechanics and diesel engine specialists	High school diploma or equivalent	Long-term on-the-job training	As fast as average	$40,000 to $59,999
Bus drivers, transit and intercity	High school diploma or equivalent	Moderate-term on-the-job training	Much faster than average	$40,000 to $59,999
Business teachers, postsecondary	Doctoral or professional degree	None	As fast as average	$80,000 or more
Butchers and meat cutters	No formal educational credential	Long-term on-the-job training	Decline	$30,000 to $39,999
Buyers and purchasing agents	Bachelor's degree	Moderate-term on-the-job training	Decline	$60,000 to $79,999
Cabinetmakers and bench carpenters	High school diploma or equivalent	Moderate-term on-the-job training	As fast as average	$30,000 to $39,999
Calibration technologists and technicians and engineering technologists and technicians, except drafters, all other	Associate's degree	None	Slower than average	$60,000 to $79,999
Camera and photographic equipment repairers	High school diploma or equivalent	Long-term on-the-job training	As fast as average	$40,000 to $59,999
Camera operators, television, video, and film	Bachelor's degree	None	Much faster than average	$40,000 to $59,999
Captains, mates, and pilots of water vessels	Postsecondary nondegree award	None	Faster than average	$60,000 to $79,999
Cardiovascular technologists and technicians	Associate's degree	None	As fast as average	$40,000 to $59,999
Career/technical education teachers, middle school	Bachelor's degree	None	As fast as average	$60,000 to $79,999
Career/technical education teachers, postsecondary	Bachelor's degree	None	Slower than average	$40,000 to $59,999

OCCUPATION	ENTRY-LEVEL EDUCATION	ON-THE-JOB TRAINING	PROJECTED GROWTH RATE	2020 MEDIAN PAY
Career/technical education teachers, secondary school	Bachelor's degree	None	As fast as average	$60,000 to $79,999
Cargo and freight agents	High school diploma or equivalent	Short-term on-the-job training	As fast as average	$40,000 to $59,999
Carpenters	High school diploma or equivalent	Apprenticeship	Slower than average	$40,000 to $59,999
Carpet installers	No formal educational credential	Short-term on-the-job training	Decline	$40,000 to $59,999
Cartographers and photogrammetrists	Bachelor's degree	None	Slower than average	$60,000 to $79,999
Cashiers	No formal educational credential	Short-term on-the-job training	Decline	Less than $30,000
Cement masons and concrete finishers	No formal educational credential	Moderate-term on-the-job training	Little or no change	$40,000 to $59,999
Chefs and head cooks	High school diploma or equivalent	None	Much faster than average	$40,000 to $59,999
Chemical engineers	Bachelor's degree	None	As fast as average	$80,000 or more
Chemical equipment operators and tenders	High school diploma or equivalent	Moderate-term on-the-job training	Decline	$40,000 to $59,999
Chemical plant and system operators	High school diploma or equivalent	Moderate-term on-the-job training	Little or no change	$60,000 to $79,999
Chemical technicians	Associate's degree	Moderate-term on-the-job training	Slower than average	$40,000 to $59,999
Chemistry teachers, postsecondary	Doctoral or professional degree	None	As fast as average	$80,000 or more
Chemists	Bachelor's degree	None	As fast as average	$60,000 to $79,999
Chief executives	Bachelor's degree	None	Decline	$80,000 or more
Child, family, and school social workers	Bachelor's degree	None	Faster than average	$40,000 to $59,999
Childcare workers	High school diploma or equivalent	Short-term on-the-job training	As fast as average	Less than $30,000
Chiropractors	Doctoral or professional degree	None	Faster than average	$60,000 to $79,999
Choreographers	High school diploma or equivalent	Long-term on-the-job training	Much faster than average	$40,000 to $59,999
Civil engineering technologists and technicians	Associate's degree	None	Slower than average	$40,000 to $59,999
Civil engineers	Bachelor's degree	None	As fast as average	$80,000 or more
Claims adjusters, examiners, and investigators	High school diploma or equivalent	Long-term on-the-job training	Decline	$60,000 to $79,999
Cleaners of vehicles and equipment	No formal educational credential	Short-term on-the-job training	As fast as average	Less than $30,000
Cleaning, washing, and metal pickling equipment operators and tenders	High school diploma or equivalent	Moderate-term on-the-job training	As fast as average	$30,000 to $39,999

OCCUPATION	ENTRY-LEVEL EDUCATION	ON-THE-JOB TRAINING	PROJECTED GROWTH RATE	2020 MEDIAN PAY
Clergy	Bachelor's degree	Moderate-term on-the-job training	Slower than average	$40,000 to $59,999
Clinical laboratory technologists and technicians	Bachelor's degree	None	Faster than average	$40,000 to $59,999
Clinical, counseling, and school psychologists	Doctoral or professional degree	Internship/ residency	As fast as average	$60,000 to $79,999
Coaches and scouts	Bachelor's degree	None	Much faster than average	$30,000 to $39,999
Coating, painting, and spraying machine setters, operators, and tenders	High school diploma or equivalent	Moderate-term on-the-job training	As fast as average	$30,000 to $39,999
Coil winders, tapers, and finishers	High school diploma or equivalent	Moderate-term on-the-job training	Decline	$30,000 to $39,999
Coin, vending, and amusement machine servicers and repairers	High school diploma or equivalent	Short-term on-the-job training	As fast as average	$30,000 to $39,999
Commercial and industrial designers	Bachelor's degree	None	As fast as average	$60,000 to $79,999
Commercial divers	Postsecondary nondegree award	Moderate-term on-the-job training	Much faster than average	$40,000 to $59,999
Commercial pilots	High school diploma or equivalent	Moderate-term on-the-job training	Faster than average	$80,000 or more
Communications equipment operators, all other	High school diploma or equivalent	Short-term on-the-job training	Faster than average	$40,000 to $59,999
Communications teachers, postsecondary	Doctoral or professional degree	None	As fast as average	$60,000 to $79,999
Community and social service specialists, all other	Bachelor's degree	None	Faster than average	$40,000 to $59,999
Community health workers	High school diploma or equivalent	Short-term on-the-job training	Much faster than average	$40,000 to $59,999
Compensation and benefits managers	Bachelor's degree	None	Slower than average	$80,000 or more
Compensation, benefits, and job analysis specialists	Bachelor's degree	None	As fast as average	$60,000 to $79,999
Compliance officers	Bachelor's degree	Moderate-term on-the-job training	As fast as average	$60,000 to $79,999
Computer and information research scientists	Master's degree	None	Much faster than average	$80,000 or more
Computer and information systems managers	Bachelor's degree	None	Faster than average	$80,000 or more
Computer hardware engineers	Bachelor's degree	None	Slower than average	$80,000 or more
Computer network architects	Bachelor's degree	None	Slower than average	$80,000 or more
Computer network support specialists	Associate's degree	None	As fast as average	$60,000 to $79,999
Computer numerically controlled tool operators	High school diploma or equivalent	Moderate-term on-the-job training	Decline	$40,000 to $59,999
Computer numerically controlled tool programmers	Postsecondary nondegree award	Moderate-term on-the-job training	Much faster than average	$40,000 to $59,999
Computer occupations, all other	Bachelor's degree	None	As fast as average	$80,000 or more
Computer programmers	Bachelor's degree	None	Decline	$80,000 or more

OCCUPATION	ENTRY-LEVEL EDUCATION	ON-THE-JOB TRAINING	PROJECTED GROWTH RATE	2020 MEDIAN PAY
Computer science teachers, postsecondary	Doctoral or professional degree	None	As fast as average	$80,000 or more
Computer systems analysts	Bachelor's degree	None	As fast as average	$80,000 or more
Computer user support specialists	Some college, no degree	None	As fast as average	$40,000 to $59,999
Computer, automated teller, and office machine repairers	Some college, no degree	Short-term on-the-job training	Decline	$40,000 to $59,999
Concierges	High school diploma or equivalent	Moderate-term on-the-job training	Much faster than average	$30,000 to $39,999
Conservation scientists	Bachelor's degree	None	As fast as average	$60,000 to $79,999
Construction and building inspectors	High school diploma or equivalent	Moderate-term on-the-job training	Decline	$60,000 to $79,999
Construction laborers	No formal educational credential	Short-term on-the-job training	As fast as average	$30,000 to $39,999
Construction managers	Bachelor's degree	Moderate-term on-the-job training	Faster than average	$80,000 or more
Continuous mining machine operators	No formal educational credential	Moderate-term on-the-job training	As fast as average	$40,000 to $59,999
Control and valve installers and repairers, except mechanical door	High school diploma or equivalent	Moderate-term on-the-job training	Slower than average	$60,000 to $79,999
Conveyor operators and tenders	No formal educational credential	Short-term on-the-job training	As fast as average	$30,000 to $39,999
Cooks, all other	No formal educational credential	Moderate-term on-the-job training	Faster than average	$30,000 to $39,999
Cooks, fast food	No formal educational credential	Short-term on-the-job training	Decline	Less than $30,000
Cooks, institution and cafeteria	No formal educational credential	Short-term on-the-job training	As fast as average	Less than $30,000
Cooks, private household	Postsecondary nondegree award	None	Slower than average	$30,000 to $39,999
Cooks, restaurant	No formal educational credential	Moderate-term on-the-job training	Much faster than average	Less than $30,000
Cooks, short order	No formal educational credential	Short-term on-the-job training	As fast as average	Less than $30,000
Cooling and freezing equipment operators and tenders	High school diploma or equivalent	Moderate-term on-the-job training	As fast as average	$30,000 to $39,999
Correctional officers and jailers	High school diploma or equivalent	Moderate-term on-the-job training	Decline	$40,000 to $59,999
Correspondence clerks	High school diploma or equivalent	Short-term on-the-job training	Decline	$30,000 to $39,999
Cost estimators	Bachelor's degree	Moderate-term on-the-job training	Little or no change	$60,000 to $79,999
Costume attendants	High school diploma or equivalent	Short-term on-the-job training	Much faster than average	$40,000 to $59,999

OCCUPATION	ENTRY-LEVEL EDUCATION	ON-THE-JOB TRAINING	PROJECTED GROWTH RATE	2020 MEDIAN PAY
Counselors, all other	Master's degree	None	As fast as average	$40,000 to $59,999
Counter and rental clerks	No formal educational credential	Short-term on-the-job training	As fast as average	$30,000 to $39,999
Couriers and messengers	High school diploma or equivalent	Short-term on-the-job training	Decline	$30,000 to $39,999
Court reporters and simultaneous captioners	Postsecondary nondegree award	Short-term on-the-job training	Slower than average	$60,000 to $79,999
Court, municipal, and license clerks	High school diploma or equivalent	Long-term on-the-job training	As fast as average	$40,000 to $59,999
Craft artists	No formal educational credential	Long-term on-the-job training	Faster than average	$30,000 to $39,999
Crane and tower operators	High school diploma or equivalent	Moderate-term on-the-job training	Slower than average	$40,000 to $59,999
Credit analysts	Bachelor's degree	None	Decline	$60,000 to $79,999
Credit authorizers, checkers, and clerks	High school diploma or equivalent	Moderate-term on-the-job training	Decline	$40,000 to $59,999
Credit counselors	Bachelor's degree	Moderate-term on-the-job training	As fast as average	$40,000 to $59,999
Crematory operators and personal care and service workers, all other	High school diploma or equivalent	Short-term on-the-job training	Much faster than average	Less than $30,000
Criminal justice and law enforcement teachers, postsecondary	Doctoral or professional degree	None	Faster than average	$60,000 to $79,999
Crossing guards and flaggers	No formal educational credential	Short-term on-the-job training	Faster than average	$30,000 to $39,999
Crushing, grinding, and polishing machine setters, operators, and tenders	High school diploma or equivalent	Moderate-term on-the-job training	Little or no change	$30,000 to $39,999
Curators	Master's degree	None	Much faster than average	$40,000 to $59,999
Customer service representatives	High school diploma or equivalent	Short-term on-the-job training	Little or no change	$30,000 to $39,999
Cutters and trimmers, hand	No formal educational credential	Short-term on-the-job training	Decline	$30,000 to $39,999
Cutting and slicing machine setters, operators, and tenders	High school diploma or equivalent	Moderate-term on-the-job training	Decline	$30,000 to $39,999
Cutting, punching, and press machine setters, operators, and tenders, metal and plastic	High school diploma or equivalent	Moderate-term on-the-job training	Decline	$30,000 to $39,999
Dancers	No formal educational credential	Long-term on-the-job training	Much faster than average	n/a
Data entry keyers	High school diploma or equivalent	Short-term on-the-job training	Decline	$30,000 to $39,999
Data scientists and mathematical science occupations, all other	Bachelor's degree	None	Much faster than average	$80,000 or more
Database administrators and architects	Bachelor's degree	None	As fast as average	$80,000 or more

OCCUPATION	ENTRY-LEVEL EDUCATION	ON-THE-JOB TRAINING	PROJECTED GROWTH RATE	2020 MEDIAN PAY
Demonstrators and product promoters	No formal educational credential	Short-term on-the-job training	As fast as average	$30,000 to $39,999
Dental assistants	Postsecondary nondegree award	None	Faster than average	$40,000 to $59,999
Dental hygienists	Associate's degree	None	Faster than average	$60,000 to $79,999
Dental laboratory technicians	High school diploma or equivalent	Moderate-term on-the-job training	Faster than average	$40,000 to $59,999
Dentists, all other specialists	Doctoral or professional degree	Internship/ residency	Slower than average	$80,000 or more
Dentists, general	Doctoral or professional degree	None	As fast as average	$80,000 or more
Derrick operators, oil and gas	No formal educational credential	Short-term on-the-job training	Much faster than average	$40,000 to $59,999
Designers, all other	Bachelor's degree	None	Little or no change	$60,000 to $79,999
Desktop publishers	Associate's degree	Short-term on-the-job training	Decline	$40,000 to $59,999
Detectives and criminal investigators	High school diploma or equivalent	Moderate-term on-the-job training	Slower than average	$80,000 or more
Diagnostic medical sonographers	Associate's degree	None	Much faster than average	$60,000 to $79,999
Dietetic technicians	Associate's degree	None	As fast as average	$30,000 to $39,999
Dietitians and nutritionists	Bachelor's degree	Internship/ residency	Faster than average	$60,000 to $79,999
Dining room and cafeteria attendants and bartender helpers	No formal educational credential	Short-term on-the-job training	Much faster than average	Less than $30,000
Directors, religious activities and education	Bachelor's degree	None	Slower than average	$40,000 to $59,999
Dishwashers	No formal educational credential	Short-term on-the-job training	Much faster than average	Less than $30,000
Dispatchers, except police, fire, and ambulance	High school diploma or equivalent	Moderate-term on-the-job training	Slower than average	$40,000 to $59,999
Door-to-door sales workers, news and street vendors, and related workers	No formal educational credential	Short-term on-the-job training	Decline	Less than $30,000
Drafters, all other	Associate's degree	None	Decline	$40,000 to $59,999
Dredge operators	High school diploma or equivalent	Moderate-term on-the-job training	Slower than average	$40,000 to $59,999
Drilling and boring machine tool setters, operators, and tenders, metal and plastic	High school diploma or equivalent	Moderate-term on-the-job training	Decline	$30,000 to $39,999
Driver/sales workers	High school diploma or equivalent	Short-term on-the-job training	Much faster than average	Less than $30,000
Drywall and ceiling tile installers	No formal educational credential	Moderate-term on-the-job training	Slower than average	$40,000 to $59,999

OCCUPATION	ENTRY-LEVEL EDUCATION	ON-THE-JOB TRAINING	PROJECTED GROWTH RATE	2020 MEDIAN PAY
Earth drillers, except oil and gas; and explosives workers, ordnance handling experts, and blasters	High school diploma or equivalent	Long-term on-the-job training	As fast as average	$40,000 to $59,999
Economics teachers, postsecondary	Doctoral or professional degree	None	As fast as average	$80,000 or more
Economists	Master's degree	None	Faster than average	$80,000 or more
Editors	Bachelor's degree	None	Slower than average	$60,000 to $79,999
Education administrators, all other	Bachelor's degree	None	Faster than average	$80,000 or more
Education administrators, kindergarten through secondary	Master's degree	None	As fast as average	$80,000 or more
Education administrators, postsecondary	Master's degree	None	As fast as average	$80,000 or more
Education and childcare administrators, preschool and daycare	Bachelor's degree	None	Faster than average	$40,000 to $59,999
Education teachers, postsecondary	Doctoral or professional degree	None	As fast as average	$60,000 to $79,999
Educational instruction and library workers, all other	Bachelor's degree	None	As fast as average	$40,000 to $59,999
Educational, guidance, and career counselors and advisors	Master's degree	None	Faster than average	$40,000 to $59,999
Electric motor, power tool, and related repairers	High school diploma or equivalent	Moderate-term on-the-job training	As fast as average	$40,000 to $59,999
Electrical and electronic engineering technologists and technicians	Associate's degree	None	Slower than average	$60,000 to $79,999
Electrical and electronics drafters	Associate's degree	None	Slower than average	$60,000 to $79,999
Electrical and electronics installers and repairers, transportation equipment	Postsecondary nondegree award	Long-term on-the-job training	As fast as average	$60,000 to $79,999
Electrical and electronics repairers, commercial and industrial equipment	Postsecondary nondegree award	Long-term on-the-job training	Slower than average	$60,000 to $79,999
Electrical and electronics repairers, powerhouse, substation, and relay	Postsecondary nondegree award	Moderate-term on-the-job training	Decline	$80,000 or more
Electrical engineers	Bachelor's degree	None	As fast as average	$80,000 or more
Electrical power-line installers and repairers	High school diploma or equivalent	Long-term on-the-job training	Little or no change	$60,000 to $79,999
Electrical, electronic, and electromechanical assemblers, except coil winders, tapers, and finishers	High school diploma or equivalent	Moderate-term on-the-job training	As fast as average	$30,000 to $39,999
Electricians	High school diploma or equivalent	Apprenticeship	As fast as average	$40,000 to $59,999
Electro-mechanical and mechatronics technologists and technicians	Associate's degree	None	Decline	$40,000 to $59,999
Electronic equipment installers and repairers, motor vehicles	High school diploma or equivalent	Moderate-term on-the-job training	Decline	$30,000 to $39,999
Electronics engineers, except computer	Bachelor's degree	None	As fast as average	$80,000 or more
Elementary school teachers, except special education	Bachelor's degree	None	As fast as average	$60,000 to $79,999

OCCUPATION	ENTRY-LEVEL EDUCATION	ON-THE-JOB TRAINING	PROJECTED GROWTH RATE	2020 MEDIAN PAY
Elevator and escalator installers and repairers	High school diploma or equivalent	Apprenticeship	As fast as average	$80,000 or more
Eligibility interviewers, government programs	High school diploma or equivalent	Moderate-term on-the-job training	Slower than average	$40,000 to $59,999
Embalmers	Associate's degree	Long-term on-the-job training	Little or no change	$40,000 to $59,999
Emergency management directors	Bachelor's degree	None	As fast as average	$60,000 to $79,999
Emergency medical technicians and paramedics	Postsecondary nondegree award	None	Faster than average	$30,000 to $39,999
Engine and other machine assemblers	High school diploma or equivalent	Moderate-term on-the-job training	Decline	$40,000 to $59,999
Engineering teachers, postsecondary	Doctoral or professional degree	None	Faster than average	$80,000 or more
Engineers, all other	Bachelor's degree	None	Slower than average	$80,000 or more
English language and literature teachers, postsecondary	Doctoral or professional degree	None	As fast as average	$60,000 to $79,999
Entertainment attendants and related workers, all other	High school diploma or equivalent	Short-term on-the-job training	Much faster than average	Less than $30,000
Environmental engineering technologists and technicians	Associate's degree	None	As fast as average	$40,000 to $59,999
Environmental engineers	Bachelor's degree	None	Slower than average	$80,000 or more
Environmental science and protection technicians, including health	Associate's degree	None	Faster than average	$40,000 to $59,999
Environmental science teachers, postsecondary	Doctoral or professional degree	None	As fast as average	$80,000 or more
Environmental scientists and specialists, including health	Bachelor's degree	None	As fast as average	$60,000 to $79,999
Epidemiologists	Master's degree	None	Much faster than average	$60,000 to $79,999
Etchers and engravers	High school diploma or equivalent	Moderate-term on-the-job training	Slower than average	$30,000 to $39,999
Excavating and loading machine and dragline operators, surface mining	High school diploma or equivalent	Moderate-term on-the-job training	Slower than average	$40,000 to $59,999
Executive secretaries and executive administrative assistants	High school diploma or equivalent	None	Decline	$60,000 to $79,999
Exercise physiologists	Bachelor's degree	None	Faster than average	$40,000 to $59,999
Exercise trainers and group fitness instructors	High school diploma or equivalent	Short-term on-the-job training	Much faster than average	$40,000 to $59,999
Extruding and drawing machine setters, operators, and tenders, metal and plastic	High school diploma or equivalent	Moderate-term on-the-job training	Decline	$30,000 to $39,999
Extruding and forming machine setters, operators, and tenders, synthetic and glass fibers	High school diploma or equivalent	Moderate-term on-the-job training	Decline	$30,000 to $39,999
Extruding, forming, pressing, and compacting machine setters, operators, and tenders	High school diploma or equivalent	Moderate-term on-the-job training	Little or no change	$30,000 to $39,999
Fabric and apparel patternmakers	High school diploma or equivalent	Moderate-term on-the-job training	Decline	$40,000 to $59,999

OCCUPATION	ENTRY-LEVEL EDUCATION	ON-THE-JOB TRAINING	PROJECTED GROWTH RATE	2020 MEDIAN PAY
Fallers	High school diploma or equivalent	Moderate-term on-the-job training	Little or no change	$40,000 to $59,999
Family and consumer sciences teachers, postsecondary	Doctoral or professional degree	None	As fast as average	$60,000 to $79,999
Family medicine physicians	Doctoral or professional degree	Internship/ residency	Slower than average	$80,000 or more
Farm and home management educators	Master's degree	None	Little or no change	$40,000 to $59,999
Farm equipment mechanics and service technicians	High school diploma or equivalent	Long-term on-the-job training	Faster than average	$40,000 to $59,999
Farm labor contractors	No formal educational credential	Short-term on-the-job training	Faster than average	$40,000 to $59,999
Farmers, ranchers, and other agricultural managers	High school diploma or equivalent	None	Little or no change	$60,000 to $79,999
Farmworkers and laborers, crop, nursery, and greenhouse	No formal educational credential	Short-term on-the-job training	Slower than average	Less than $30,000
Farmworkers, farm, ranch, and aquacultural animals	No formal educational credential	Short-term on-the-job training	Decline	Less than $30,000
Fashion designers	Bachelor's degree	None	Little or no change	$60,000 to $79,999
Fast food and counter workers	No formal educational credential	Short-term on-the-job training	Faster than average	Less than $30,000
Fence erectors	No formal educational credential	Moderate-term on-the-job training	Slower than average	$30,000 to $39,999
Fiberglass laminators and fabricators	High school diploma or equivalent	Moderate-term on-the-job training	Little or no change	$30,000 to $39,999
File clerks	High school diploma or equivalent	Short-term on-the-job training	Decline	$30,000 to $39,999
Film and video editors	Bachelor's degree	None	Much faster than average	$60,000 to $79,999
Financial and investment analysts, financial risk specialists, and financial specialists, all other	Bachelor's degree	None	As fast as average	$80,000 or more
Financial clerks, all other	High school diploma or equivalent	Short-term on-the-job training	As fast as average	$40,000 to $59,999
Financial examiners	Bachelor's degree	Long-term on-the-job training	Much faster than average	$80,000 or more
Financial managers	Bachelor's degree	None	Much faster than average	$80,000 or more
Fine artists, including painters, sculptors, and illustrators	Bachelor's degree	Long-term on-the-job training	Much faster than average	$40,000 to $59,999
Fire inspectors and investigators	Postsecondary nondegree award	Moderate-term on-the-job training	As fast as average	$60,000 to $79,999
Firefighters	Postsecondary nondegree award	Long-term on-the-job training	As fast as average	$40,000 to $59,999
First-line supervisors of construction trades and extraction workers	High school diploma or equivalent	None	As fast as average	$60,000 to $79,999
First-line supervisors of correctional officers	High school diploma or equivalent	None	Decline	$60,000 to $79,999

OCCUPATION	ENTRY-LEVEL EDUCATION	ON-THE-JOB TRAINING	PROJECTED GROWTH RATE	2020 MEDIAN PAY
First-line supervisors of farming, fishing, and forestry workers	High school diploma or equivalent	None	As fast as average	$40,000 to $59,999
First-line supervisors of firefighting and prevention workers	Postsecondary nondegree award	Moderate-term on-the-job training	As fast as average	$60,000 to $79,999
First-line supervisors of food preparation and serving workers	High school diploma or equivalent	None	Much faster than average	$30,000 to $39,999
First-line supervisors of gambling services workers	High school diploma or equivalent	None	Much faster than average	$40,000 to $59,999
First-line supervisors of housekeeping and janitorial workers	High school diploma or equivalent	None	As fast as average	$40,000 to $59,999
First-line supervisors of landscaping, lawn service, and groundskeeping workers	High school diploma or equivalent	None	Slower than average	$40,000 to $59,999
First-line supervisors of mechanics, installers, and repairers	High school diploma or equivalent	None	As fast as average	$60,000 to $79,999
First-line supervisors of non-retail sales workers	High school diploma or equivalent	None	Decline	$60,000 to $79,999
First-line supervisors of office and administrative support workers	High school diploma or equivalent	None	Decline	$40,000 to $59,999
First-line supervisors of personal service and entertainment and recreation workers, except gambling services	High school diploma or equivalent	None	Much faster than average	$40,000 to $59,999
First-line supervisors of police and detectives	High school diploma or equivalent	Moderate-term on-the-job training	As fast as average	$80,000 or more
First-line supervisors of production and operating workers	High school diploma or equivalent	None	Slower than average	$60,000 to $79,999
First-line supervisors of retail sales workers	High school diploma or equivalent	None	Decline	$40,000 to $59,999
First-line supervisors of transportation and material-moving workers, except aircraft cargo handling supervisors	High school diploma or equivalent	None	As fast as average	$40,000 to $59,999
Fish and game wardens	Bachelor's degree	Moderate-term on-the-job training	Little or no change	$40,000 to $59,999
Fishing and hunting workers	No formal educational credential	Moderate-term on-the-job training	Faster than average	n/a
Flight attendants	High school diploma or equivalent	Moderate-term on-the-job training	Much faster than average	$40,000 to $59,999
Floor layers, except carpet, wood, and hard tiles	No formal educational credential	Moderate-term on-the-job training	Faster than average	$40,000 to $59,999
Floor sanders and finishers	No formal educational credential	Moderate-term on-the-job training	Slower than average	$30,000 to $39,999
Floral designers	High school diploma or equivalent	Moderate-term on-the-job training	Decline	Less than $30,000
Food and tobacco roasting, baking, and drying machine operators and tenders	No formal educational credential	Moderate-term on-the-job training	Slower than average	$30,000 to $39,999
Food batchmakers	High school diploma or equivalent	Moderate-term on-the-job training	As fast as average	$30,000 to $39,999
Food cooking machine operators and tenders	High school diploma or equivalent	Moderate-term on-the-job training	Slower than average	$30,000 to $39,999

OCCUPATION	ENTRY-LEVEL EDUCATION	ON-THE-JOB TRAINING	PROJECTED GROWTH RATE	2020 MEDIAN PAY
Food preparation and serving related workers, all other	No formal educational credential	Short-term on-the-job training	Much faster than average	Less than $30,000
Food preparation workers	No formal educational credential	Short-term on-the-job training	As fast as average	Less than $30,000
Food processing workers, all other	No formal educational credential	Moderate-term on-the-job training	Slower than average	Less than $30,000
Food scientists and technologists	Bachelor's degree	None	As fast as average	$60,000 to $79,999
Food servers, nonrestaurant	No formal educational credential	Short-term on-the-job training	Faster than average	Less than $30,000
Food service managers	High school diploma or equivalent	None	Faster than average	$40,000 to $59,999
Foreign language and literature teachers, postsecondary	Doctoral or professional degree	None	As fast as average	$60,000 to $79,999
Forensic science technicians	Bachelor's degree	Moderate-term on-the-job training	Much faster than average	$60,000 to $79,999
Forest and conservation technicians	Associate's degree	None	Little or no change	$30,000 to $39,999
Forest and conservation workers	High school diploma or equivalent	Moderate-term on-the-job training	Decline	$30,000 to $39,999
Forest fire inspectors and prevention specialists	High school diploma or equivalent	Moderate-term on-the-job training	Much faster than average	$40,000 to $59,999
Foresters	Bachelor's degree	None	As fast as average	$60,000 to $79,999
Forestry and conservation science teachers, postsecondary	Doctoral or professional degree	None	As fast as average	$80,000 or more
Forging machine setters, operators, and tenders, metal and plastic	High school diploma or equivalent	Moderate-term on-the-job training	Decline	$40,000 to $59,999
Foundry mold and coremakers	High school diploma or equivalent	Moderate-term on-the-job training	Decline	$30,000 to $39,999
Fundraisers	Bachelor's degree	None	Much faster than average	$40,000 to $59,999
Funeral attendants	High school diploma or equivalent	Short-term on-the-job training	Slower than average	Less than $30,000
Funeral home managers	Associate's degree	None	Slower than average	$60,000 to $79,999
Furnace, kiln, oven, drier, and kettle operators and tenders	High school diploma or equivalent	Moderate-term on-the-job training	Slower than average	$40,000 to $59,999
Furniture finishers	High school diploma or equivalent	Short-term on-the-job training	As fast as average	$30,000 to $39,999
Gambling and sports book writers and runners	High school diploma or equivalent	Short-term on-the-job training	Much faster than average	Less than $30,000
Gambling cage workers	High school diploma or equivalent	Short-term on-the-job training	Much faster than average	Less than $30,000
Gambling change persons and booth cashiers	No formal educational credential	Short-term on-the-job training	Much faster than average	Less than $30,000
Gambling dealers	High school diploma or equivalent	Short-term on-the-job training	Much faster than average	Less than $30,000

OCCUPATION	ENTRY-LEVEL EDUCATION	ON-THE-JOB TRAINING	PROJECTED GROWTH RATE	2020 MEDIAN PAY
Gambling managers	High school diploma or equivalent	None	Much faster than average	$60,000 to $79,999
Gambling service workers, all other	High school diploma or equivalent	Short-term on-the-job training	Much faster than average	Less than $30,000
Gambling surveillance officers and gambling investigators	High school diploma or equivalent	Moderate-term on-the-job training	Faster than average	$30,000 to $39,999
Gas compressor and gas pumping station operators	High school diploma or equivalent	Moderate-term on-the-job training	Little or no change	$60,000 to $79,999
Gas plant operators	High school diploma or equivalent	Long-term on-the-job training	Decline	$60,000 to $79,999
General and operations managers	Bachelor's degree	None	As fast as average	$80,000 or more
General internal medicine physicians	Doctoral or professional degree	Internship/residency	Little or no change	$80,000 or more
Genetic counselors	Master's degree	None	Much faster than average	$80,000 or more
Geographers	Bachelor's degree	None	Little or no change	$80,000 or more
Geography teachers, postsecondary	Doctoral or professional degree	None	As fast as average	$80,000 or more
Geological and hydrologic technicians	Associate's degree	Moderate-term on-the-job training	As fast as average	$40,000 to $59,999
Geoscientists, except hydrologists and geographers	Bachelor's degree	None	As fast as average	$80,000 or more
Glaziers	High school diploma or equivalent	Apprenticeship	Slower than average	$40,000 to $59,999
Graders and sorters, agricultural products	No formal educational credential	Short-term on-the-job training	Little or no change	Less than $30,000
Graphic designers	Bachelor's degree	None	Slower than average	$40,000 to $59,999
Grinding and polishing workers, hand	No formal educational credential	Moderate-term on-the-job training	Decline	$30,000 to $39,999
Grinding, lapping, polishing, and buffing machine tool setters, operators, and tenders, metal and plastic	High school diploma or equivalent	Moderate-term on-the-job training	Decline	$30,000 to $39,999
Grounds maintenance workers, all other	No formal educational credential	Short-term on-the-job training	As fast as average	$30,000 to $39,999
Hairdressers, hairstylists, and cosmetologists	Postsecondary nondegree award	None	Much faster than average	Less than $30,000
Hazardous materials removal workers	High school diploma or equivalent	Moderate-term on-the-job training	As fast as average	$40,000 to $59,999
Health and safety engineers, except mining safety engineers and inspectors	Bachelor's degree	None	As fast as average	$80,000 or more
Health education specialists	Bachelor's degree	None	Faster than average	$40,000 to $59,999
Health information technologists, medical registrars, surgical assistants, and healthcare practitioners and technical workers, all other	Postsecondary nondegree award	None	Faster than average	$40,000 to $59,999
Health specialties teachers, postsecondary	Doctoral or professional degree	None	Much faster than average	$80,000 or more

OCCUPATION	ENTRY-LEVEL EDUCATION	ON-THE-JOB TRAINING	PROJECTED GROWTH RATE	2020 MEDIAN PAY
Healthcare social workers	Master's degree	Internship/residency	Faster than average	$40,000 to $59,999
Healthcare support workers, all other	High school diploma or equivalent	None	Faster than average	$30,000 to $39,999
Hearing aid specialists	High school diploma or equivalent	Moderate-term on-the-job training	Faster than average	$40,000 to $59,999
Heat treating equipment setters, operators, and tenders, metal and plastic	High school diploma or equivalent	Moderate-term on-the-job training	Decline	$30,000 to $39,999
Heating, air conditioning, and refrigeration mechanics and installers	Postsecondary nondegree award	Long-term on-the-job training	Slower than average	$40,000 to $59,999
Heavy and tractor-trailer truck drivers	Postsecondary nondegree award	Short-term on-the-job training	As fast as average	$40,000 to $59,999
Helpers, construction trades, all other	No formal educational credential	Short-term on-the-job training	As fast as average	$30,000 to $39,999
Helpers--brickmasons, blockmasons, stonemasons, and tile and marble setters	No formal educational credential	Short-term on-the-job training	Decline	$30,000 to $39,999
Helpers--carpenters	No formal educational credential	Short-term on-the-job training	Little or no change	$30,000 to $39,999
Helpers--electricians	High school diploma or equivalent	Short-term on-the-job training	Little or no change	$30,000 to $39,999
Helpers--extraction workers	High school diploma or equivalent	Moderate-term on-the-job training	Much faster than average	$30,000 to $39,999
Helpers--installation, maintenance, and repair workers	High school diploma or equivalent	Short-term on-the-job training	As fast as average	$30,000 to $39,999
Helpers--painters, paperhangers, plasterers, and stucco masons	No formal educational credential	Short-term on-the-job training	As fast as average	$30,000 to $39,999
Helpers--pipelayers, plumbers, pipefitters, and steamfitters	High school diploma or equivalent	Short-term on-the-job training	As fast as average	$30,000 to $39,999
Helpers--production workers	High school diploma or equivalent	Short-term on-the-job training	Decline	$30,000 to $39,999
Helpers--roofers	No formal educational credential	Short-term on-the-job training	Slower than average	$30,000 to $39,999
Highway maintenance workers	High school diploma or equivalent	Moderate-term on-the-job training	As fast as average	$40,000 to $59,999
Historians	Master's degree	None	Slower than average	$60,000 to $79,999
History teachers, postsecondary	Doctoral or professional degree	None	As fast as average	$60,000 to $79,999
Hoist and winch operators	No formal educational credential	Short-term on-the-job training	Slower than average	$60,000 to $79,999
Home appliance repairers	High school diploma or equivalent	Moderate-term on-the-job training	Decline	$40,000 to $59,999
Home health and personal care aides	High school diploma or equivalent	Short-term on-the-job training	Much faster than average	Less than $30,000
Hosts and hostesses, restaurant, lounge, and coffee shop	No formal educational credential	Short-term on-the-job training	Much faster than average	Less than $30,000

OCCUPATION	ENTRY-LEVEL EDUCATION	ON-THE-JOB TRAINING	PROJECTED GROWTH RATE	2020 MEDIAN PAY
Hotel, motel, and resort desk clerks	High school diploma or equivalent	Short-term on-the-job training	Much faster than average	Less than $30,000
Human resources assistants, except payroll and timekeeping	Associate's degree	None	Decline	$40,000 to $59,999
Human resources managers	Bachelor's degree	None	As fast as average	$80,000 or more
Human resources specialists	Bachelor's degree	None	As fast as average	$60,000 to $79,999
Hydrologists	Bachelor's degree	None	As fast as average	$80,000 or more
Industrial engineering technologists and technicians	Associate's degree	None	Slower than average	$40,000 to $59,999
Industrial engineers	Bachelor's degree	None	Faster than average	$80,000 or more
Industrial machinery mechanics	High school diploma or equivalent	Long-term on-the-job training	Much faster than average	$40,000 to $59,999
Industrial production managers	Bachelor's degree	None	Slower than average	$80,000 or more
Industrial truck and tractor operators	No formal educational credential	Short-term on-the-job training	As fast as average	$30,000 to $39,999
Industrial-organizational psychologists	Master's degree	Internship/residency	Slower than average	$80,000 or more
Information and record clerks, all other	High school diploma or equivalent	Short-term on-the-job training	Slower than average	$40,000 to $59,999
Information security analysts	Bachelor's degree	None	Much faster than average	$80,000 or more
Inspectors, testers, sorters, samplers, and weighers	High school diploma or equivalent	Moderate-term on-the-job training	Decline	$40,000 to $59,999
Installation, maintenance, and repair workers, all other	High school diploma or equivalent	Moderate-term on-the-job training	As fast as average	$40,000 to $59,999
Instructional coordinators	Master's degree	None	As fast as average	$60,000 to $79,999
Insulation workers, floor, ceiling, and wall	No formal educational credential	Short-term on-the-job training	Slower than average	$40,000 to $59,999
Insulation workers, mechanical	High school diploma or equivalent	Apprenticeship	Slower than average	$40,000 to $59,999
Insurance appraisers, auto damage	Postsecondary nondegree award	Moderate-term on-the-job training	Little or no change	$60,000 to $79,999
Insurance claims and policy processing clerks	High school diploma or equivalent	Moderate-term on-the-job training	Little or no change	$40,000 to $59,999
Insurance sales agents	High school diploma or equivalent	Moderate-term on-the-job training	As fast as average	$40,000 to $59,999
Insurance underwriters	Bachelor's degree	Moderate-term on-the-job training	Decline	$60,000 to $79,999
Interior designers	Bachelor's degree	None	Little or no change	$40,000 to $59,999
Interpreters and translators	Bachelor's degree	None	Much faster than average	$40,000 to $59,999
Interviewers, except eligibility and loan	High school diploma or equivalent	Short-term on-the-job training	Decline	$30,000 to $39,999

OCCUPATION	ENTRY-LEVEL EDUCATION	ON-THE-JOB TRAINING	PROJECTED GROWTH RATE	2020 MEDIAN PAY
Janitors and cleaners, except maids and housekeeping cleaners	No formal educational credential	Short-term on-the-job training	As fast as average	Less than $30,000
Jewelers and precious stone and metal workers	High school diploma or equivalent	Long-term on-the-job training	Little or no change	$40,000 to $59,999
Judges, magistrate judges, and magistrates	Doctoral or professional degree	Short-term on-the-job training	Slower than average	$80,000 or more
Judicial law clerks	Doctoral or professional degree	None	Slower than average	$40,000 to $59,999
Kindergarten teachers, except special education	Bachelor's degree	None	As fast as average	$40,000 to $59,999
Labor relations specialists	Bachelor's degree	None	Decline	$60,000 to $79,999
Laborers and freight, stock, and material movers, hand	No formal educational credential	Short-term on-the-job training	As fast as average	$30,000 to $39,999
Landscape architects	Bachelor's degree	Internship/ residency	Little or no change	$60,000 to $79,999
Landscaping and groundskeeping workers	No formal educational credential	Short-term on-the-job training	As fast as average	$30,000 to $39,999
Lathe and turning machine tool setters, operators, and tenders, metal and plastic	High school diploma or equivalent	Moderate-term on-the-job training	Decline	$40,000 to $59,999
Laundry and dry-cleaning workers	No formal educational credential	Short-term on-the-job training	Faster than average	Less than $30,000
Law teachers, postsecondary	Doctoral or professional degree	None	Faster than average	$80,000 or more
Lawyers	Doctoral or professional degree	None	As fast as average	$80,000 or more
Layout workers, metal and plastic	High school diploma or equivalent	Moderate-term on-the-job training	Decline	$40,000 to $59,999
Legal secretaries and administrative assistants	High school diploma or equivalent	Moderate-term on-the-job training	Decline	$40,000 to $59,999
Legal support workers, all other	Associate's degree	None	Little or no change	$40,000 to $59,999
Legislators	Bachelor's degree	None	As fast as average	$30,000 to $39,999
Librarians and media collections specialists	Master's degree	None	As fast as average	$60,000 to $79,999
Library assistants, clerical	High school diploma or equivalent	Short-term on-the-job training	Little or no change	Less than $30,000
Library science teachers, postsecondary	Doctoral or professional degree	None	As fast as average	$60,000 to $79,999
Library technicians	Postsecondary nondegree award	None	Little or no change	$30,000 to $39,999
Licensed practical and licensed vocational nurses	Postsecondary nondegree award	None	As fast as average	$40,000 to $59,999
Life scientists, all other	Bachelor's degree	None	As fast as average	$80,000 or more
Life, physical, and social science technicians, all other	Associate's degree	None	As fast as average	$40,000 to $59,999

OCCUPATION	ENTRY-LEVEL EDUCATION	ON-THE-JOB TRAINING	PROJECTED GROWTH RATE	2020 MEDIAN PAY
Lifeguards, ski patrol, and other recreational protective service workers	No formal educational credential	Short-term on-the-job training	Much faster than average	Less than $30,000
Light truck drivers	High school diploma or equivalent	Short-term on-the-job training	As fast as average	$30,000 to $39,999
Lighting technicians and media and communication equipment workers, all other	High school diploma or equivalent	Short-term on-the-job training	Much faster than average	$60,000 to $79,999
Loading and moving machine operators, underground mining	No formal educational credential	Short-term on-the-job training	Decline	$40,000 to $59,999
Loan interviewers and clerks	High school diploma or equivalent	Short-term on-the-job training	Decline	$40,000 to $59,999
Loan officers	Bachelor's degree	Moderate-term on-the-job training	Little or no change	$60,000 to $79,999
Locker room, coatroom, and dressing room attendants	High school diploma or equivalent	Short-term on-the-job training	Much faster than average	Less than $30,000
Locksmiths and safe repairers	High school diploma or equivalent	Long-term on-the-job training	Decline	$40,000 to $59,999
Locomotive engineers	High school diploma or equivalent	Moderate-term on-the-job training	As fast as average	$60,000 to $79,999
Lodging managers	High school diploma or equivalent	None	As fast as average	$40,000 to $59,999
Log graders and scalers	High school diploma or equivalent	Moderate-term on-the-job training	As fast as average	$30,000 to $39,999
Logging equipment operators	High school diploma or equivalent	Moderate-term on-the-job training	As fast as average	$40,000 to $59,999
Logging workers, all other	High school diploma or equivalent	Moderate-term on-the-job training	As fast as average	$40,000 to $59,999
Logisticians	Bachelor's degree	None	Much faster than average	$60,000 to $79,999
Machine feeders and offbearers	No formal educational credential	Short-term on-the-job training	As fast as average	$30,000 to $39,999
Machinists	High school diploma or equivalent	Long-term on-the-job training	As fast as average	$40,000 to $59,999
Magnetic resonance imaging technologists	Associate's degree	None	As fast as average	$60,000 to $79,999
Maids and housekeeping cleaners	No formal educational credential	Short-term on-the-job training	Faster than average	Less than $30,000
Mail clerks and mail machine operators, except postal service	High school diploma or equivalent	Short-term on-the-job training	Decline	$30,000 to $39,999
Maintenance and repair workers, general	High school diploma or equivalent	Moderate-term on-the-job training	As fast as average	$40,000 to $59,999
Maintenance workers, machinery	High school diploma or equivalent	Long-term on-the-job training	Faster than average	$40,000 to $59,999
Makeup artists, theatrical and performance	Postsecondary nondegree award	None	Much faster than average	$80,000 or more
Management analysts	Bachelor's degree	None	Faster than average	$80,000 or more
Manicurists and pedicurists	Postsecondary nondegree award	None	Much faster than average	Less than $30,000

OCCUPATION	ENTRY-LEVEL EDUCATION	ON-THE-JOB TRAINING	PROJECTED GROWTH RATE	2020 MEDIAN PAY
Manufactured building and mobile home installers	High school diploma or equivalent	Short-term on-the-job training	Decline	$30,000 to $39,999
Marine engineers and naval architects	Bachelor's degree	None	Slower than average	$80,000 or more
Market research analysts and marketing specialists	Bachelor's degree	None	Much faster than average	$60,000 to $79,999
Marketing managers	Bachelor's degree	None	As fast as average	$80,000 or more
Marriage and family therapists	Master's degree	Internship/ residency	Much faster than average	$40,000 to $59,999
Massage therapists	Postsecondary nondegree award	None	Much faster than average	$40,000 to $59,999
Material moving workers, all other	No formal educational credential	Short-term on-the-job training	As fast as average	$30,000 to $39,999
Materials engineers	Bachelor's degree	None	As fast as average	$80,000 or more
Materials scientists	Bachelor's degree	None	Slower than average	$80,000 or more
Mathematical science teachers, postsecondary	Doctoral or professional degree	None	As fast as average	$60,000 to $79,999
Mathematicians	Master's degree	None	Slower than average	$80,000 or more
Meat, poultry, and fish cutters and trimmers	No formal educational credential	Short-term on-the-job training	Slower than average	$30,000 to $39,999
Mechanical door repairers	High school diploma or equivalent	Moderate-term on-the-job training	Faster than average	$40,000 to $59,999
Mechanical drafters	Associate's degree	None	Decline	$40,000 to $59,999
Mechanical engineering technologists and technicians	Associate's degree	None	As fast as average	$40,000 to $59,999
Mechanical engineers	Bachelor's degree	None	As fast as average	$80,000 or more
Media and communication workers, all other	High school diploma or equivalent	Short-term on-the-job training	Much faster than average	$40,000 to $59,999
Medical and health services managers	Bachelor's degree	None	Much faster than average	$80,000 or more
Medical appliance technicians	High school diploma or equivalent	Moderate-term on-the-job training	Faster than average	$40,000 to $59,999
Medical assistants	Postsecondary nondegree award	None	Much faster than average	$30,000 to $39,999
Medical dosimetrists, medical records specialists, and health technologists and technicians, all other	Postsecondary nondegree award	None	As fast as average	$40,000 to $59,999
Medical equipment preparers	High school diploma or equivalent	Moderate-term on-the-job training	As fast as average	$30,000 to $39,999
Medical equipment repairers	Associate's degree	Moderate-term on-the-job training	As fast as average	$40,000 to $59,999
Medical scientists, except epidemiologists	Doctoral or professional degree	None	Much faster than average	$80,000 or more
Medical secretaries and administrative assistants	High school diploma or equivalent	Moderate-term on-the-job training	Faster than average	$30,000 to $39,999

OCCUPATION	ENTRY-LEVEL EDUCATION	ON-THE-JOB TRAINING	PROJECTED GROWTH RATE	2020 MEDIAN PAY
Medical transcriptionists	Postsecondary nondegree award	None	Decline	$30,000 to $39,999
Meeting, convention, and event planners	Bachelor's degree	None	Much faster than average	$40,000 to $59,999
Mental health and substance abuse social workers	Master's degree	Internship/residency	Faster than average	$40,000 to $59,999
Merchandise displayers and window trimmers	High school diploma or equivalent	Short-term on-the-job training	Slower than average	$30,000 to $39,999
Metal workers and plastic workers, all other	High school diploma or equivalent	Moderate-term on-the-job training	Decline	$30,000 to $39,999
Metal-refining furnace operators and tenders	High school diploma or equivalent	Moderate-term on-the-job training	Slower than average	$40,000 to $59,999
Meter readers, utilities	High school diploma or equivalent	Short-term on-the-job training	Decline	$40,000 to $59,999
Microbiologists	Bachelor's degree	None	Slower than average	$80,000 or more
Middle school teachers, except special and career/technical education	Bachelor's degree	None	As fast as average	$60,000 to $79,999
Milling and planing machine setters, operators, and tenders, metal and plastic	High school diploma or equivalent	Moderate-term on-the-job training	Decline	$40,000 to $59,999
Millwrights	High school diploma or equivalent	Apprenticeship	As fast as average	$40,000 to $59,999
Mining and geological engineers, including mining safety engineers	Bachelor's degree	None	Slower than average	$80,000 or more
Miscellaneous assemblers and fabricators	High school diploma or equivalent	Moderate-term on-the-job training	Decline	$30,000 to $39,999
Miscellaneous construction and related workers	High school diploma or equivalent	Moderate-term on-the-job training	As fast as average	$30,000 to $39,999
Miscellaneous entertainers and performers, sports and related workers	No formal educational credential	Short-term on-the-job training	Much faster than average	n/a
Miscellaneous first-line supervisors, protective service workers	High school diploma or equivalent	None	As fast as average	$40,000 to $59,999
Mixing and blending machine setters, operators, and tenders	High school diploma or equivalent	Moderate-term on-the-job training	Slower than average	$30,000 to $39,999
Mobile heavy equipment mechanics, except engines	High school diploma or equivalent	Long-term on-the-job training	Faster than average	$40,000 to $59,999
Model makers, metal and plastic	High school diploma or equivalent	Moderate-term on-the-job training	Decline	$40,000 to $59,999
Model makers, wood	High school diploma or equivalent	Moderate-term on-the-job training	Much faster than average	$60,000 to $79,999
Models	No formal educational credential	None	Faster than average	$30,000 to $39,999
Molders, shapers, and casters, except metal and plastic	High school diploma or equivalent	Long-term on-the-job training	Faster than average	$30,000 to $39,999
Molding, coremaking, and casting machine setters, operators, and tenders, metal and plastic	High school diploma or equivalent	Moderate-term on-the-job training	Decline	$30,000 to $39,999
Morticians, undertakers, and funeral arrangers	Associate's degree	Long-term on-the-job training	Slower than average	$40,000 to $59,999

OCCUPATION	ENTRY-LEVEL EDUCATION	ON-THE-JOB TRAINING	PROJECTED GROWTH RATE	2020 MEDIAN PAY
Motion picture projectionists	No formal educational credential	Short-term on-the-job training	Much faster than average	Less than $30,000
Motor vehicle operators, all other	No formal educational credential	Short-term on-the-job training	As fast as average	$30,000 to $39,999
Motorboat mechanics and service technicians	High school diploma or equivalent	Long-term on-the-job training	Faster than average	$40,000 to $59,999
Motorboat operators	Postsecondary nondegree award	None	Faster than average	$40,000 to $59,999
Motorcycle mechanics	Postsecondary nondegree award	Short-term on-the-job training	As fast as average	$30,000 to $39,999
Multiple machine tool setters, operators, and tenders, metal and plastic	High school diploma or equivalent	Moderate-term on-the-job training	As fast as average	$30,000 to $39,999
Museum technicians and conservators	Bachelor's degree	None	Much faster than average	$40,000 to $59,999
Music directors and composers	Bachelor's degree	None	As fast as average	$40,000 to $59,999
Musical instrument repairers and tuners	High school diploma or equivalent	Apprenticeship	Decline	$30,000 to $39,999
Musicians and singers	No formal educational credential	Long-term on-the-job training	Faster than average	n/a
Natural sciences managers	Bachelor's degree	None	As fast as average	$80,000 or more
Network and computer systems administrators	Bachelor's degree	None	Slower than average	$80,000 or more
New accounts clerks	High school diploma or equivalent	Moderate-term on-the-job training	Decline	$30,000 to $39,999
News analysts, reporters, and journalists	Bachelor's degree	None	As fast as average	$40,000 to $59,999
Nuclear engineers	Bachelor's degree	None	Decline	$80,000 or more
Nuclear medicine technologists	Associate's degree	None	As fast as average	$60,000 to $79,999
Nuclear power reactor operators	High school diploma or equivalent	Long-term on-the-job training	Decline	$80,000 or more
Nuclear technicians	Associate's degree	Moderate-term on-the-job training	Decline	$80,000 or more
Nurse anesthetists	Master's degree	None	Faster than average	$80,000 or more
Nurse midwives	Master's degree	None	Faster than average	$80,000 or more
Nurse practitioners	Master's degree	None	Much faster than average	$80,000 or more
Nursing assistants	Postsecondary nondegree award	None	As fast as average	$30,000 to $39,999
Nursing instructors and teachers, postsecondary	Doctoral or professional degree	None	Much faster than average	$60,000 to $79,999
Obstetricians and gynecologists	Doctoral or professional degree	Internship/ residency	Decline	$80,000 or more
Occupational health and safety specialists	Bachelor's degree	None	As fast as average	$60,000 to $79,999

OCCUPATION	ENTRY-LEVEL EDUCATION	ON-THE-JOB TRAINING	PROJECTED GROWTH RATE	2020 MEDIAN PAY
Occupational health and safety technicians	High school diploma or equivalent	Moderate-term on-the-job training	As fast as average	$40,000 to $59,999
Occupational therapists	Master's degree	None	Much faster than average	$80,000 or more
Occupational therapy aides	High school diploma or equivalent	Short-term on-the-job training	Much faster than average	$30,000 to $39,999
Occupational therapy assistants	Associate's degree	None	Much faster than average	$60,000 to $79,999
Office and administrative support workers, all other	High school diploma or equivalent	Short-term on-the-job training	As fast as average	$30,000 to $39,999
Office clerks, general	High school diploma or equivalent	Short-term on-the-job training	Decline	$30,000 to $39,999
Office machine operators, except computer	High school diploma or equivalent	Short-term on-the-job training	Decline	$30,000 to $39,999
Operating engineers and other construction equipment operators	High school diploma or equivalent	Moderate-term on-the-job training	Slower than average	$40,000 to $59,999
Operations research analysts	Bachelor's degree	None	Much faster than average	$80,000 or more
Ophthalmic laboratory technicians	High school diploma or equivalent	Moderate-term on-the-job training	Faster than average	$30,000 to $39,999
Ophthalmic medical technicians	Postsecondary nondegree award	None	Faster than average	$30,000 to $39,999
Opticians, dispensing	High school diploma or equivalent	Long-term on-the-job training	As fast as average	$30,000 to $39,999
Optometrists	Doctoral or professional degree	None	As fast as average	$80,000 or more
Oral and maxillofacial surgeons	Doctoral or professional degree	Internship/residency	As fast as average	$80,000 or more
Order clerks	Some college, no degree	Short-term on-the-job training	Decline	$30,000 to $39,999
Orderlies	High school diploma or equivalent	Short-term on-the-job training	As fast as average	$30,000 to $39,999
Orthodontists	Doctoral or professional degree	Internship/residency	As fast as average	$80,000 or more
Orthotists and prosthetists	Master's degree	Internship/residency	Much faster than average	$60,000 to $79,999
Outdoor power equipment and other small engine mechanics	High school diploma or equivalent	Moderate-term on-the-job training	As fast as average	$30,000 to $39,999
Packaging and filling machine operators and tenders	High school diploma or equivalent	Moderate-term on-the-job training	Slower than average	$30,000 to $39,999
Packers and packagers, hand	No formal educational credential	Short-term on-the-job training	Little or no change	Less than $30,000
Painters, construction and maintenance	No formal educational credential	Moderate-term on-the-job training	Slower than average	$40,000 to $59,999
Painting, coating, and decorating workers	No formal educational credential	Moderate-term on-the-job training	As fast as average	$30,000 to $39,999
Paper goods machine setters, operators, and tenders	High school diploma or equivalent	Moderate-term on-the-job training	Decline	$30,000 to $39,999

OCCUPATION	ENTRY-LEVEL EDUCATION	ON-THE-JOB TRAINING	PROJECTED GROWTH RATE	2020 MEDIAN PAY
Paperhangers	No formal educational credential	Long-term on-the-job training	As fast as average	$40,000 to $59,999
Paralegals and legal assistants	Associate's degree	None	Faster than average	$40,000 to $59,999
Parking attendants	No formal educational credential	Short-term on-the-job training	Faster than average	Less than $30,000
Parking enforcement workers	High school diploma or equivalent	Short-term on-the-job training	Decline	$40,000 to $59,999
Parts salespersons	No formal educational credential	Moderate-term on-the-job training	Slower than average	$30,000 to $39,999
Passenger attendants	High school diploma or equivalent	Short-term on-the-job training	Much faster than average	Less than $30,000
Passenger vehicle drivers, except bus drivers, transit and intercity	No formal educational credential	Short-term on-the-job training	Much faster than average	$30,000 to $39,999
Patternmakers, metal and plastic	High school diploma or equivalent	Moderate-term on-the-job training	Decline	$40,000 to $59,999
Patternmakers, wood	High school diploma or equivalent	Moderate-term on-the-job training	Much faster than average	$60,000 to $79,999
Paving, surfacing, and tamping equipment operators	High school diploma or equivalent	Moderate-term on-the-job training	As fast as average	$40,000 to $59,999
Payroll and timekeeping clerks	High school diploma or equivalent	Moderate-term on-the-job training	Decline	$40,000 to $59,999
Pediatricians, general	Doctoral or professional degree	Internship/ residency	Decline	$80,000 or more
Personal financial advisors	Bachelor's degree	Long-term on-the-job training	Slower than average	$80,000 or more
Personal service managers, all other; entertainment and recreation managers, except gambling; and managers, all other	Bachelor's degree	None	As fast as average	$80,000 or more
Pest control workers	High school diploma or equivalent	Moderate-term on-the-job training	As fast as average	$30,000 to $39,999
Pesticide handlers, sprayers, and applicators, vegetation	High school diploma or equivalent	Moderate-term on-the-job training	As fast as average	$30,000 to $39,999
Petroleum engineers	Bachelor's degree	None	As fast as average	$80,000 or more
Petroleum pump system operators, refinery operators, and gaugers	High school diploma or equivalent	Moderate-term on-the-job training	As fast as average	$60,000 to $79,999
Pharmacists	Doctoral or professional degree	None	Decline	$80,000 or more
Pharmacy aides	High school diploma or equivalent	Short-term on-the-job training	Decline	Less than $30,000
Pharmacy technicians	High school diploma or equivalent	Moderate-term on-the-job training	Slower than average	$30,000 to $39,999
Philosophy and religion teachers, postsecondary	Doctoral or professional degree	None	Faster than average	$60,000 to $79,999
Phlebotomists	Postsecondary nondegree award	None	Much faster than average	$30,000 to $39,999
Photographers	High school diploma or equivalent	Moderate-term on-the-job training	Much faster than average	$40,000 to $59,999

OCCUPATION	ENTRY-LEVEL EDUCATION	ON-THE-JOB TRAINING	PROJECTED GROWTH RATE	2020 MEDIAN PAY
Photographic process workers and processing machine operators	High school diploma or equivalent	Short-term on-the-job training	Decline	$30,000 to $39,999
Physical scientists, all other	Bachelor's degree	None	Little or no change	$80,000 or more
Physical therapist aides	High school diploma or equivalent	Short-term on-the-job training	Much faster than average	Less than $30,000
Physical therapist assistants	Associate's degree	None	Much faster than average	$40,000 to $59,999
Physical therapists	Doctoral or professional degree	None	Much faster than average	$80,000 or more
Physician assistants	Master's degree	None	Much faster than average	$80,000 or more
Physicians, all other; and ophthalmologists, except pediatric	Doctoral or professional degree	Internship/ residency	Slower than average	$80,000 or more
Physicists	Doctoral or professional degree	None	As fast as average	$80,000 or more
Physics teachers, postsecondary	Doctoral or professional degree	None	As fast as average	$80,000 or more
Pile driver operators	High school diploma or equivalent	Moderate-term on-the-job training	Slower than average	$60,000 to $79,999
Pipelayers	No formal educational credential	Short-term on-the-job training	Little or no change	$40,000 to $59,999
Plant and system operators, all other	High school diploma or equivalent	Moderate-term on-the-job training	Slower than average	$40,000 to $59,999
Plasterers and stucco masons	No formal educational credential	Long-term on-the-job training	As fast as average	$40,000 to $59,999
Plating machine setters, operators, and tenders, metal and plastic	High school diploma or equivalent	Moderate-term on-the-job training	Decline	$30,000 to $39,999
Plumbers, pipefitters, and steamfitters	High school diploma or equivalent	Apprenticeship	Slower than average	$40,000 to $59,999
Podiatrists	Doctoral or professional degree	Internship/ residency	Slower than average	$80,000 or more
Police and sheriff's patrol officers	High school diploma or equivalent	Moderate-term on-the-job training	As fast as average	$60,000 to $79,999
Political science teachers, postsecondary	Doctoral or professional degree	None	As fast as average	$80,000 or more
Political scientists	Master's degree	None	As fast as average	$80,000 or more
Postal service clerks	High school diploma or equivalent	Short-term on-the-job training	Decline	$40,000 to $59,999
Postal service mail carriers	High school diploma or equivalent	Short-term on-the-job training	Decline	$40,000 to $59,999
Postal service mail sorters, processors, and processing machine operators	High school diploma or equivalent	Short-term on-the-job training	Decline	$40,000 to $59,999
Postmasters and mail superintendents	High school diploma or equivalent	Moderate-term on-the-job training	Decline	$60,000 to $79,999
Postsecondary teachers, all other	Doctoral or professional degree	None	As fast as average	$60,000 to $79,999
Pourers and casters, metal	High school diploma or equivalent	Moderate-term on-the-job training	Decline	$40,000 to $59,999

OCCUPATION	ENTRY-LEVEL EDUCATION	ON-THE-JOB TRAINING	PROJECTED GROWTH RATE	2020 MEDIAN PAY
Power distributors and dispatchers	High school diploma or equivalent	Long-term on-the-job training	Decline	$80,000 or more
Power plant operators	High school diploma or equivalent	Long-term on-the-job training	Decline	$80,000 or more
Precision instrument and equipment repairers, all other	High school diploma or equivalent	Long-term on-the-job training	As fast as average	$60,000 to $79,999
Prepress technicians and workers	Postsecondary nondegree award	None	Decline	$40,000 to $59,999
Preschool teachers, except special education	Associate's degree	None	Much faster than average	$30,000 to $39,999
Pressers, textile, garment, and related materials	No formal educational credential	Short-term on-the-job training	Decline	Less than $30,000
Print binding and finishing workers	High school diploma or equivalent	Moderate-term on-the-job training	Decline	$30,000 to $39,999
Printing press operators	High school diploma or equivalent	Moderate-term on-the-job training	Decline	$30,000 to $39,999
Private detectives and investigators	High school diploma or equivalent	Moderate-term on-the-job training	Faster than average	$40,000 to $59,999
Probation officers and correctional treatment specialists	Bachelor's degree	Short-term on-the-job training	Slower than average	$40,000 to $59,999
Procurement clerks	High school diploma or equivalent	Moderate-term on-the-job training	Decline	$40,000 to $59,999
Producers and directors	Bachelor's degree	None	Much faster than average	$60,000 to $79,999
Production workers, all other	High school diploma or equivalent	Moderate-term on-the-job training	As fast as average	$30,000 to $39,999
Production, planning, and expediting clerks	High school diploma or equivalent	Moderate-term on-the-job training	As fast as average	$40,000 to $59,999
Project management specialists and business operations specialists, all other	Bachelor's degree	None	As fast as average	$60,000 to $79,999
Proofreaders and copy markers	Bachelor's degree	None	Slower than average	$40,000 to $59,999
Property appraisers and assessors	Bachelor's degree	Long-term on-the-job training	Slower than average	$40,000 to $59,999
Property, real estate, and community association managers	High school diploma or equivalent	None	Slower than average	$40,000 to $59,999
Prosthodontists	Doctoral or professional degree	Internship/ residency	As fast as average	$80,000 or more
Psychiatric aides	High school diploma or equivalent	Short-term on-the-job training	As fast as average	$30,000 to $39,999
Psychiatric technicians	Postsecondary nondegree award	Short-term on-the-job training	Faster than average	$30,000 to $39,999
Psychiatrists	Doctoral or professional degree	Internship/ residency	Faster than average	$80,000 or more
Psychologists, all other	Master's degree	Internship/ residency	Slower than average	$80,000 or more
Psychology teachers, postsecondary	Doctoral or professional degree	None	As fast as average	$60,000 to $79,999
Public relations and fundraising managers	Bachelor's degree	None	Faster than average	$80,000 or more
Public relations specialists	Bachelor's degree	None	Faster than average	$60,000 to $79,999

OCCUPATION	ENTRY-LEVEL EDUCATION	ON-THE-JOB TRAINING	PROJECTED GROWTH RATE	2020 MEDIAN PAY
Public safety telecommunicators	High school diploma or equivalent	Moderate-term on-the-job training	As fast as average	$40,000 to $59,999
Pump operators, except wellhead pumpers	High school diploma or equivalent	Moderate-term on-the-job training	Faster than average	$40,000 to $59,999
Purchasing managers	Bachelor's degree	None	As fast as average	$80,000 or more
Radiation therapists	Associate's degree	None	As fast as average	$80,000 or more
Radio, cellular, and tower equipment installers and repairers	Associate's degree	Moderate-term on-the-job training	Slower than average	$40,000 to $59,999
Radiologic technologists and technicians	Associate's degree	None	As fast as average	$60,000 to $79,999
Rail car repairers	High school diploma or equivalent	Long-term on-the-job training	Slower than average	$40,000 to $59,999
Rail transportation workers, all other	High school diploma or equivalent	Moderate-term on-the-job training	Slower than average	$40,000 to $59,999
Rail yard engineers, dinkey operators, and hostlers	High school diploma or equivalent	Moderate-term on-the-job training	Little or no change	$40,000 to $59,999
Rail-track laying and maintenance equipment operators	High school diploma or equivalent	Moderate-term on-the-job training	Slower than average	$40,000 to $59,999
Railroad brake, signal, and switch operators and locomotive firers	High school diploma or equivalent	Moderate-term on-the-job training	Slower than average	$40,000 to $59,999
Railroad conductors and yardmasters	High school diploma or equivalent	Moderate-term on-the-job training	As fast as average	$60,000 to $79,999
Real estate brokers	High school diploma or equivalent	None	Slower than average	$60,000 to $79,999
Real estate sales agents	High school diploma or equivalent	Moderate-term on-the-job training	Slower than average	$40,000 to $59,999
Receptionists and information clerks	High school diploma or equivalent	Short-term on-the-job training	Slower than average	$30,000 to $39,999
Recreation and fitness studies teachers, postsecondary	Doctoral or professional degree	None	As fast as average	$60,000 to $79,999
Recreation workers	High school diploma or equivalent	Short-term on-the-job training	Much faster than average	Less than $30,000
Recreational therapists	Bachelor's degree	None	As fast as average	$40,000 to $59,999
Recreational vehicle service technicians	High school diploma or equivalent	Long-term on-the-job training	Much faster than average	$40,000 to $59,999
Refractory materials repairers, except brickmasons	High school diploma or equivalent	Moderate-term on-the-job training	Decline	$40,000 to $59,999
Refuse and recyclable material collectors	No formal educational credential	Short-term on-the-job training	Faster than average	$30,000 to $39,999
Registered nurses	Bachelor's degree	None	As fast as average	$60,000 to $79,999
Rehabilitation counselors	Master's degree	None	As fast as average	$30,000 to $39,999
Reinforcing iron and rebar workers	High school diploma or equivalent	Apprenticeship	Slower than average	$40,000 to $59,999
Religious workers, all other	Bachelor's degree	None	Slower than average	$30,000 to $39,999
Reservation and transportation ticket agents and travel clerks	High school diploma or equivalent	Short-term on-the-job training	Faster than average	$30,000 to $39,999

OCCUPATION	ENTRY-LEVEL EDUCATION	ON-THE-JOB TRAINING	PROJECTED GROWTH RATE	2020 MEDIAN PAY
Residential advisors	High school diploma or equivalent	Short-term on-the-job training	Faster than average	$30,000 to $39,999
Respiratory therapists	Associate's degree	None	Much faster than average	$60,000 to $79,999
Retail salespersons	No formal educational credential	Short-term on-the-job training	Little or no change	Less than $30,000
Riggers	High school diploma or equivalent	Moderate-term on-the-job training	Faster than average	$40,000 to $59,999
Rock splitters, quarry	No formal educational credential	Short-term on-the-job training	As fast as average	$30,000 to $39,999
Rolling machine setters, operators, and tenders, metal and plastic	High school diploma or equivalent	Moderate-term on-the-job training	Decline	$40,000 to $59,999
Roof bolters, mining	High school diploma or equivalent	Moderate-term on-the-job training	Decline	$60,000 to $79,999
Roofers	No formal educational credential	Moderate-term on-the-job training	Slower than average	$40,000 to $59,999
Rotary drill operators, oil and gas	No formal educational credential	Moderate-term on-the-job training	Much faster than average	$40,000 to $59,999
Roustabouts, oil and gas	No formal educational credential	Moderate-term on-the-job training	Much faster than average	$30,000 to $39,999
Sailors and marine oilers	No formal educational credential	Moderate-term on-the-job training	As fast as average	$40,000 to $59,999
Sales and related workers, all other	High school diploma or equivalent	None	Slower than average	$30,000 to $39,999
Sales engineers	Bachelor's degree	Moderate-term on-the-job training	As fast as average	$80,000 or more
Sales managers	Bachelor's degree	None	As fast as average	$80,000 or more
Sales representatives of services, except advertising, insurance, financial services, and travel	High school diploma or equivalent	Moderate-term on-the-job training	As fast as average	$40,000 to $59,999
Sales representatives, wholesale and manufacturing, except technical and scientific products	High school diploma or equivalent	Moderate-term on-the-job training	Slower than average	$60,000 to $79,999
Sales representatives, wholesale and manufacturing, technical and scientific products	Bachelor's degree	Moderate-term on-the-job training	As fast as average	$80,000 or more
Sawing machine setters, operators, and tenders, wood	High school diploma or equivalent	Moderate-term on-the-job training	As fast as average	$30,000 to $39,999
School bus monitors and protective service workers, all other	High school diploma or equivalent	Short-term on-the-job training	Faster than average	$30,000 to $39,999
Secondary school teachers, except special and career/technical education	Bachelor's degree	None	As fast as average	$60,000 to $79,999
Secretaries and administrative assistants, except legal, medical, and executive	High school diploma or equivalent	Short-term on-the-job training	Decline	$30,000 to $39,999
Securities, commodities, and financial services sales agents	Bachelor's degree	Moderate-term on-the-job training	Slower than average	$60,000 to $79,999

OCCUPATION	ENTRY-LEVEL EDUCATION	ON-THE-JOB TRAINING	PROJECTED GROWTH RATE	2020 MEDIAN PAY
Security and fire alarm systems installers	High school diploma or equivalent	Moderate-term on-the-job training	Much faster than average	$40,000 to $59,999
Security guards	High school diploma or equivalent	Short-term on-the-job training	Faster than average	$30,000 to $39,999
Self-enrichment teachers	High school diploma or equivalent	None	Much faster than average	$30,000 to $39,999
Semiconductor processing technicians	High school diploma or equivalent	Moderate-term on-the-job training	Decline	$40,000 to $59,999
Separating, filtering, clarifying, precipitating, and still machine setters, operators, and tenders	High school diploma or equivalent	Moderate-term on-the-job training	Slower than average	$40,000 to $59,999
Septic tank servicers and sewer pipe cleaners	High school diploma or equivalent	Moderate-term on-the-job training	Faster than average	$40,000 to $59,999
Service unit operators, oil and gas	No formal educational credential	Moderate-term on-the-job training	Much faster than average	$40,000 to $59,999
Set and exhibit designers	Bachelor's degree	None	As fast as average	$40,000 to $59,999
Sewers, hand	No formal educational credential	Moderate-term on-the-job training	Decline	$30,000 to $39,999
Sewing machine operators	No formal educational credential	Short-term on-the-job training	Decline	Less than $30,000
Shampooers	No formal educational credential	Short-term on-the-job training	Much faster than average	Less than $30,000
Sheet metal workers	High school diploma or equivalent	Apprenticeship	Slower than average	$40,000 to $59,999
Ship engineers	Postsecondary nondegree award	None	As fast as average	$60,000 to $79,999
Shipping, receiving, and inventory clerks	High school diploma or equivalent	Short-term on-the-job training	Decline	$30,000 to $39,999
Shoe and leather workers and repairers	High school diploma or equivalent	Moderate-term on-the-job training	Decline	$30,000 to $39,999
Shoe machine operators and tenders	High school diploma or equivalent	Short-term on-the-job training	Decline	$30,000 to $39,999
Signal and track switch repairers	High school diploma or equivalent	Moderate-term on-the-job training	As fast as average	$60,000 to $79,999
Skincare specialists	Postsecondary nondegree award	None	Much faster than average	$30,000 to $39,999
Slaughterers and meat packers	No formal educational credential	Short-term on-the-job training	Slower than average	$30,000 to $39,999
Social and community service managers	Bachelor's degree	None	Faster than average	$60,000 to $79,999
Social and human service assistants	High school diploma or equivalent	Short-term on-the-job training	Much faster than average	$30,000 to $39,999
Social science research assistants	Bachelor's degree	None	As fast as average	$40,000 to $59,999
Social sciences teachers, postsecondary, all other	Doctoral or professional degree	None	Slower than average	$60,000 to $79,999
Social scientists and related workers, all other	Bachelor's degree	None	Slower than average	$80,000 or more

OCCUPATION	ENTRY-LEVEL EDUCATION	ON-THE-JOB TRAINING	PROJECTED GROWTH RATE	2020 MEDIAN PAY
Social work teachers, postsecondary	Doctoral or professional degree	None	As fast as average	$60,000 to $79,999
Social workers, all other	Bachelor's degree	None	As fast as average	$60,000 to $79,999
Sociologists	Master's degree	None	Slower than average	$80,000 or more
Sociology teachers, postsecondary	Doctoral or professional degree	None	As fast as average	$60,000 to $79,999
Software developers and software quality assurance analysts and testers	Bachelor's degree	None	Much faster than average	$80,000 or more
Soil and plant scientists	Bachelor's degree	None	As fast as average	$60,000 to $79,999
Solar photovoltaic installers	High school diploma or equivalent	Moderate-term on-the-job training	Much faster than average	$40,000 to $59,999
Sound engineering technicians	Postsecondary nondegree award	Short-term on-the-job training	Much faster than average	$40,000 to $59,999
Special education teachers, all other	Bachelor's degree	None	Faster than average	$60,000 to $79,999
Special education teachers, kindergarten and elementary school	Bachelor's degree	None	As fast as average	$60,000 to $79,999
Special education teachers, middle school	Bachelor's degree	None	As fast as average	$60,000 to $79,999
Special education teachers, preschool	Bachelor's degree	None	Faster than average	$60,000 to $79,999
Special education teachers, secondary school	Bachelor's degree	None	As fast as average	$60,000 to $79,999
Special effects artists and animators	Bachelor's degree	None	Much faster than average	$60,000 to $79,999
Speech-language pathologists	Master's degree	Internship/ residency	Much faster than average	$80,000 or more
Stationary engineers and boiler operators	High school diploma or equivalent	Long-term on-the-job training	As fast as average	$60,000 to $79,999
Statistical assistants	Bachelor's degree	None	As fast as average	$40,000 to $59,999
Statisticians	Master's degree	None	Much faster than average	$80,000 or more
Stockers and order fillers	High school diploma or equivalent	Short-term on-the-job training	Slower than average	Less than $30,000
Stonemasons	High school diploma or equivalent	Apprenticeship	Little or no change	$40,000 to $59,999
Structural iron and steel workers	High school diploma or equivalent	Apprenticeship	As fast as average	$40,000 to $59,999
Structural metal fabricators and fitters	High school diploma or equivalent	Moderate-term on-the-job training	Decline	$40,000 to $59,999
Substance abuse, behavioral disorder, and mental health counselors	Bachelor's degree	None	Much faster than average	$40,000 to $59,999
Substitute teachers, short-term	Bachelor's degree	None	Faster than average	Less than $30,000
Subway and streetcar operators	High school diploma or equivalent	Moderate-term on-the-job training	As fast as average	$60,000 to $79,999
Surgeons, except ophthalmologists	Doctoral or professional degree	Internship/ residency	Decline	$80,000 or more

OCCUPATION	ENTRY-LEVEL EDUCATION	ON-THE-JOB TRAINING	PROJECTED GROWTH RATE	2020 MEDIAN PAY
Surgical technologists	Postsecondary nondegree award	None	As fast as average	$40,000 to $59,999
Survey researchers	Master's degree	None	Slower than average	$40,000 to $59,999
Surveying and mapping technicians	High school diploma or equivalent	Moderate-term on-the-job training	Slower than average	$40,000 to $59,999
Surveyors	Bachelor's degree	Internship/ residency	Slower than average	$60,000 to $79,999
Switchboard operators, including answering service	High school diploma or equivalent	Short-term on-the-job training	Decline	$30,000 to $39,999
Tailors, dressmakers, and custom sewers	No formal educational credential	Moderate-term on-the-job training	Decline	$30,000 to $39,999
Tank car, truck, and ship loaders	No formal educational credential	Short-term on-the-job training	Slower than average	$40,000 to $59,999
Tapers	No formal educational credential	Moderate-term on-the-job training	Little or no change	$40,000 to $59,999
Tax examiners and collectors, and revenue agents	Bachelor's degree	Moderate-term on-the-job training	Decline	$40,000 to $59,999
Tax preparers	High school diploma or equivalent	Moderate-term on-the-job training	Slower than average	$40,000 to $59,999
Teaching assistants, except postsecondary	Some college, no degree	None	As fast as average	Less than $30,000
Teaching assistants, postsecondary	Bachelor's degree	None	As fast as average	$30,000 to $39,999
Technical writers	Bachelor's degree	Short-term on-the-job training	Faster than average	$60,000 to $79,999
Telecommunications equipment installers and repairers, except line installers	Postsecondary nondegree award	Moderate-term on-the-job training	Little or no change	$60,000 to $79,999
Telecommunications line installers and repairers	High school diploma or equivalent	Long-term on-the-job training	Little or no change	$40,000 to $59,999
Telemarketers	No formal educational credential	Short-term on-the-job training	Decline	Less than $30,000
Telephone operators	High school diploma or equivalent	Short-term on-the-job training	Decline	$30,000 to $39,999
Tellers	High school diploma or equivalent	Short-term on-the-job training	Decline	$30,000 to $39,999
Terrazzo workers and finishers	High school diploma or equivalent	Apprenticeship	Decline	$40,000 to $59,999
Textile bleaching and dyeing machine operators and tenders	High school diploma or equivalent	Short-term on-the-job training	Decline	$30,000 to $39,999
Textile cutting machine setters, operators, and tenders	High school diploma or equivalent	Moderate-term on-the-job training	Decline	Less than $30,000
Textile knitting and weaving machine setters, operators, and tenders	High school diploma or equivalent	Short-term on-the-job training	Decline	$30,000 to $39,999
Textile winding, twisting, and drawing out machine setters, operators, and tenders	High school diploma or equivalent	Moderate-term on-the-job training	Decline	$30,000 to $39,999
Textile, apparel, and furnishings workers, all other	High school diploma or equivalent	Short-term on-the-job training	Decline	Less than $30,000

OCCUPATION	ENTRY-LEVEL EDUCATION	ON-THE-JOB TRAINING	PROJECTED GROWTH RATE	2020 MEDIAN PAY
Therapists, all other	Bachelor's degree	None	Faster than average	$40,000 to $59,999
Tile and stone setters	No formal educational credential	Long-term on-the-job training	Faster than average	$40,000 to $59,999
Timing device assemblers and adjusters	High school diploma or equivalent	Moderate-term on-the-job training	Decline	$30,000 to $39,999
Tire builders	High school diploma or equivalent	Moderate-term on-the-job training	Little or no change	$40,000 to $59,999
Tire repairers and changers	High school diploma or equivalent	Short-term on-the-job training	Slower than average	$30,000 to $39,999
Title examiners, abstractors, and searchers	High school diploma or equivalent	Moderate-term on-the-job training	Slower than average	$40,000 to $59,999
Tool and die makers	Postsecondary nondegree award	Long-term on-the-job training	Slower than average	$40,000 to $59,999
Tool grinders, filers, and sharpeners	High school diploma or equivalent	Moderate-term on-the-job training	Decline	$40,000 to $59,999
Tour and travel guides	High school diploma or equivalent	Moderate-term on-the-job training	Much faster than average	Less than $30,000
Traffic technicians	High school diploma or equivalent	Moderate-term on-the-job training	As fast as average	$40,000 to $59,999
Training and development managers	Bachelor's degree	None	Faster than average	$80,000 or more
Training and development specialists	Bachelor's degree	None	Faster than average	$60,000 to $79,999
Transit and railroad police	High school diploma or equivalent	Moderate-term on-the-job training	As fast as average	$60,000 to $79,999
Transportation inspectors	High school diploma or equivalent	Moderate-term on-the-job training	Slower than average	$60,000 to $79,999
Transportation security screeners	High school diploma or equivalent	Short-term on-the-job training	Little or no change	$40,000 to $59,999
Transportation, storage, and distribution managers	High school diploma or equivalent	None	As fast as average	$80,000 or more
Travel agents	High school diploma or equivalent	Moderate-term on-the-job training	Slower than average	$40,000 to $59,999
Tree trimmers and pruners	High school diploma or equivalent	Short-term on-the-job training	As fast as average	$40,000 to $59,999
Tutors and teachers and instructors, all other	Bachelor's degree	None	Much faster than average	$40,000 to $59,999
Umpires, referees, and other sports officials	High school diploma or equivalent	Moderate-term on-the-job training	Much faster than average	Less than $30,000
Underground mining machine operators and extraction workers, all other	High school diploma or equivalent	Moderate-term on-the-job training	As fast as average	$40,000 to $59,999
Upholsterers	High school diploma or equivalent	Moderate-term on-the-job training	Slower than average	$30,000 to $39,999
Urban and regional planners	Master's degree	None	As fast as average	$60,000 to $79,999
Ushers, lobby attendants, and ticket takers	No formal educational credential	Short-term on-the-job training	Much faster than average	Less than $30,000
Veterinarians	Doctoral or professional degree	None	Much faster than average	$80,000 or more

OCCUPATION	ENTRY-LEVEL EDUCATION	ON-THE-JOB TRAINING	PROJECTED GROWTH RATE	2020 MEDIAN PAY
Veterinary assistants and laboratory animal caretakers	High school diploma or equivalent	Short-term on-the-job training	Faster than average	Less than $30,000
Veterinary technologists and technicians	Associate's degree	None	Faster than average	$30,000 to $39,999
Waiters and waitresses	No formal educational credential	Short-term on-the-job training	Much faster than average	Less than $30,000
Watch and clock repairers	High school diploma or equivalent	Long-term on-the-job training	Decline	$40,000 to $59,999
Water and wastewater treatment plant and system operators	High school diploma or equivalent	Long-term on-the-job training	Decline	$40,000 to $59,999
Web developers and digital interface designers	Bachelor's degree	None	Faster than average	$60,000 to $79,999
Weighers, measurers, checkers, and samplers, recordkeeping	High school diploma or equivalent	Short-term on-the-job training	Faster than average	$30,000 to $39,999
Welders, cutters, solderers, and brazers	High school diploma or equivalent	Moderate-term on-the-job training	As fast as average	$40,000 to $59,999
Welding, soldering, and brazing machine setters, operators, and tenders	High school diploma or equivalent	Moderate-term on-the-job training	Little or no change	$30,000 to $39,999
Wellhead pumpers	High school diploma or equivalent	Moderate-term on-the-job training	As fast as average	$60,000 to $79,999
Wind turbine service technicians	Postsecondary nondegree award	Long-term on-the-job training	Much faster than average	$40,000 to $59,999
Woodworkers, all other	High school diploma or equivalent	Moderate-term on-the-job training	Much faster than average	$30,000 to $39,999
Woodworking machine setters, operators, and tenders, except sawing	High school diploma or equivalent	Moderate-term on-the-job training	As fast as average	$30,000 to $39,999
Word processors and typists	High school diploma or equivalent	Short-term on-the-job training	Decline	$40,000 to $59,999
Writers and authors	Bachelor's degree	Long-term on-the-job training	As fast as average	$60,000 to $79,999
Zoologists and wildlife biologists	Bachelor's degree	None	Slower than average	$60,000 to $79,999

Source: https://www.bls.gov/ooh/occupation-finder.htm
Last Modified Date: Wednesday, September 8, 2021
n/a = The annual wage is not available.

Glossary

This glossary contains the most important terms used in this publication.

Interest	An amount, usually a percentage, that you pay to the lender for use of funds.
Subsidized Federal Student Loans	Loans on which the government pays the interest while you are a student.
Loan Consolidation	A method of combining loans to gain a common interest rate and eliminated the need to pay multiple bills.
Grace Period	The time between when you status changes and when you must begin repaying a loan.
Prepayment Penalty	Charge for paying off a loan early; lenders must disclose penalties in the terms of a loan.
Income-driven Repayment Plans	Monthly repayments are based on income—people who make less pay less. For example, on some plans, the borrower pays 10 percent of discretionary income, or what is left after paying taxes and necessary bills, such as rent.
Graduated Repayment Plans	The monthly repayments increase over the life of the loan period.
Discharge of Loans	You are no longer obligated to pay a loan if it is discharged.
Forgiveness of Loans	When a loan is forgiven, you do not have to pay the remaining balance.
Deferment	A temporary delay in making payments, sometimes permitted by loan servicers due to hardship, such as the loss of a job.
Forbearance	A temporary halt or reduction in payments due to financial hardship or illness.

SOURCES

https://studentloanhero.com/featured/5-banks-to-refinance-your-student-loans/

https://www.nerdwallet.com/blog/refinancing-student-loans/

https://studentaid.ed.gov/sa/sites/default/files/responsible-borrower.pdf

https://www.nerdwallet.com/blog/finance/what-is-a-debt-avalanche/

https://studentaid.ed.gov/sa/repay-loans/understand

http://www.feedthepig.org/master-credit-debt/student-loans#.WKydlW8rKpo

https://studentloanhero.com/featured/public-service-loan-forgiveness-do-you-qualify/

http://www.usnews.com/education/best-colleges/paying-for-college/articles/2016-06-06/8-facts-about-direct-student-loan-consolidation

https://studentaid.ed.gov/sa/node/594/#pros-cons

https://studentloans.gov/myDirectLoan/ibrInstructions.action?source=15SPRRPMT#

https://studentaid.ed.gov/sa/repay-loans/understand/plans/income-driven

https://www.dailyworth.com/posts/4228-learn-about-employer-student-loan-repayment-setalvad

http://www.forbes.com/sites/kaytiezimmerman/2016/08/23/which-employers-are-helping-millennials-repay-student-loans/#38ea4b2a9ea3

https://www.newamerica.org/education-policy/edcentral/state-loan-programs/

https://blog.ed.gov/2016/05/8-common-student-loan-mistakes/

http://www.finaid.org/loans/

https://www.debt.org/students/types-of-loans/

https://studentaid.ed.gov/sa/repay-loans

https://studentaid.ed.gov/sa/repay-loans/forgiveness-cancellation

https://turbotax.intuit.com/tax-tools/tax-tips/Tax-Deductions-and-Credits/About-Student-Loan-Tax-Credits/INF14771.html

https://nces.ed.gov/fastfacts/display.asp?id=77

https://studentloanhero.com/featured/ultimate-guide-paying-off-student-loans-faster/

https://www.debt.org/students/types-of-loans/

https://studentaid.ed.gov/sa/types/loans

https://studentaid.ed.gov/sa/types/loans/federal-vs-private

http://www.gocollege.com/financial-aid/student-loans/states/

https://www.goodcall.com/education/graduate-debt-free/

https://www.debt.org/students/student-loan-repayment-benefit/

https://studentaid.ed.gov/sa/fafsa

https://lendedu.com/blog/average-cost-of-college-statistics/

https://studentaid.ed.gov/sa/prepare-for-college/choosing-schools

https://greyhouse.weissratings.com

The Weiss Financial Ratings Series, published by Weiss Ratings and Grey House Publishing, offers libraries, schools, universities and the business community a wide range of investing, banking, insurance and financial literacy tools. Visit www.greyhouse.com or https://greyhouse.weissratings.com for more information about the titles and online tools below.

- Weiss Ratings Financial Literacy Basics
- Weiss Ratings Financial Literacy: Planning For the Future
- Weiss Ratings Financial Literacy: How to Become an Investor
- Weiss Ratings Guide to Banks
- Weiss Ratings Guide to Credit Unions
- Weiss Ratings Guide to Health Insurers
- Weiss Ratings Guide to Property & Casualty Insurers
- Weiss Ratings Guide to Life & Annuity Insurers
- Weiss Ratings Investment Research Guide to Stocks
- Weiss Ratings Investment Research Guide to Bond & Money Market Mutual Funds
- Weiss Ratings Investment Research Guide to Stock Mutual Funds
- Weiss Ratings Investment Research Guide to Exchange-Traded Funds
- Weiss Ratings Consumer Guides
- Weiss Ratings Medicare Supplement Insurance Buyers Guide
- Weiss Financial Ratings Online – **https://greyhouse.weissratings.com**